Thanks for keeping our pla

we gallivanted around NZ

your turn!

Zach + Heather

Jan '26.

REVISED AND UPDATED

NEW ZEALAND'S GREAT WALKS

THE COMPLETE GUIDE

Paul Hersey

Dunedin-based author and photographer Paul Hersey has climbed, surfed, mountain-biked, kayaked or otherwise explored his way through most corners of New Zealand and many destinations overseas. Between adventures, he researches and writes articles for various magazines, including *Alpinist*, *The Surfer's Journal*, *New Zealand Geographic* and *North & South*, and has authored several books, including *Searching for Groundswell*, *High Misadventure*, *Our Mountains* and *Merino Country*.

Shelley Hersey

Shelley Hersey has been tramping and climbing throughout New Zealand and many places overseas for the past 25 years. A former teacher, and a passionate conservationist, she currently works as an online educator delivering virtual field trips to schools.

REVISED AND UPDATED

NEW ZEALAND'S GREAT WALKS

THE COMPLETE GUIDE

PAUL AND SHELLEY HERSEY

RANDOM HOUSE
NEW ZEALAND

RANDOM HOUSE

UK | USA | Canada | Ireland | Australia
India | New Zealand | South Africa | China

Random House is an imprint of the Penguin Random House group of companies,
whose addresses can be found at global.penguinrandomhouse.com.

Penguin
Random House
New Zealand

First published by Penguin Random House New Zealand, 2018.
Reprinted and updated 2020.

3 5 7 9 10 8 6 4

The New Zealand outdoors environment is always changing. Readers are encouraged to use careful judgement at all times while tramping the Great Walks and to err on the side of caution if at all unsure about conditions. Safety should be the number-one priority.

While every effort has been made to ensure that the information in this book was accurate at the time of publication, the authors and the publisher accept no responsibility or liability for any accident or injury associated with its use. If in doubt, seek medical advice before undertaking any extended walk or similar outdoors activity.

If any errors are noted in the descriptions and information provided in this publication, please contact the publisher.

Maps in this book are intended as general guides only. For more detail, consult the recommended maps.

All photographs by Paul and Shelley Hersey unless credited otherwise
Maps by Geographx Ltd
Elevation profiles by Rachel Clark and Jono Stone
Photographs on pages 19 and 21 supplied by Bivouac Outdoor
Photograph on page 66 supplied by Ben Watson
Photographs on pages 214-15 and 226–7 supplied by Rob Suisted/www.naturespic.com

Design by Rachel Clark © Penguin Random House New Zealand
Prepress by Image Centre Group
Printed and bound in China by RR Donnelley Asia Printing Solutions Ltd

A catalogue record for this book is available from the National Library of New Zealand.

ISBN 978-0-14-377410-5

penguin.co.nz

FSC
www.fsc.org
MIX
Paper | Supporting responsible forestry
FSC® C144853

CONTENTS

PREFACE

Welcome to the Great Walks of Aotearoa New Zealand!

We hope that you enjoy the experience of travelling along these special pathways as much as we do. This book will help guide your journey; a reliable companion as you enjoy the walks. The information within these pages highlights not only how to get the most out of each trip but also how to understand better what it is you are experiencing. And, if you feel so inclined, how to share in the legacy by giving back to the environment.

If you have travelled from overseas we welcome you to Aotearoa, the Land of the Long White Cloud. Breathe. Open your eyes and your mind. Take the first of many steps. And if you are a Kiwi finally venturing out on a track you have heard so much about, well done and it's about time!

May you be blessed with warm days and star-filled evenings. Embrace the rain when it inevitably arrives. Listen for the nightly call of the kiwi, our national bird, and wake at dawn to a cacophony of song from tūī and bellbirds. Rise refreshed, only to end the day with rewarding aches in your muscles that come from time well spent.

We believe that New Zealand's Great Walks, along with the rest of our national parks, reserves and untarnished back country, are precious beyond belief. Pockets of quiet paradise are becoming more difficult to find in a busying world. So we ask you to treat them with the respect they deserve. We offer no apology for feeling so protective of what is such a beautiful taonga (treasure). As you walk (or cycle or kayak) each of these tracks or waterways, consider how much ongoing effort and care is required to ensure the landscape remains safe from overuse and development. Keep your footsteps light.

Travel well.

Paul and Shelley Hersey

INTRODUCTION

New Zealand currently has 10 Great Walks (one of which is actually a Great River Journey). In a country with hundreds of tracks these are considered the best of the best, in that they pass through some of our most spectacular landscapes, have a range of comfortable huts and campsites to stay at and are maintained to a high standard.

The Great Walks range in length from 32 to 82 kilometres, and normally take between two and six days to complete (although some are done in a day by those crazy long-distance runners!). The Whanganui Journey – on a river – is 145 kilometres long and takes up to five days to paddle by canoe or kayak.

Apart from the Waikaremoana Track and the Whanganui Journey, both of which are in the North Island and have their own status (this will be explained later), the other Great Walks fall under the umbrella of our extensive national park network. Tongariro was this country's first national park; indeed, it was one of the first in the world. In 1887, the summits of the peaks were gifted to the Crown in what was termed a tuku whenua, or land transaction, by the great chief Horonuku Te Heuheu Tūkino, in a bid to preserve the peaks' spiritual significance. The park has been expanded massively since that first gift, and now has World Heritage status.

Today there are 13 national parks spread throughout the country. Overall, New Zealand has around 10,000 protected places covering more than 8.6 million hectares. This means that about a third of our land area lies within the protective banners of the 1977 Reserves Act and the 1980 National Parks Act. Within these special areas, natural and cultural resources, along with a varied biodiversity, are preserved, maintained and managed. To many Kiwis, having so much of our precious land coming under this protection is what helps give New Zealand its distinctive character. And, to some, it is essential to our way of life.

All of the Great Walks, other than the coastal Abel Tasman track at the top of the South Island, are at least partially located in hilly country or alpine areas. New Zealand is considered a mountainous land, with three-quarters of the country lying more than 200 metres above sea level. And it is a land of constant change. Through millions of years of folding and faulting along

In 1642, the explorer Abel Tasman sailed past the land that would later become a national park named after him.

the Pacific and Indo-Australian tectonic plates, of uplifting the terrain and then eroding it down again, our landscape has been shaped both by the deep forces of the world and by the local climate.

Through these evolving and varied landscapes pass our Great Walks. Only the Tongariro Northern Circuit, which crosses a moonlike, volcanic landscape in the middle of the North Island, and the alpine Kepler Track near the bottom of the South Island are complete circuit tracks. All of the other Great Walks are through tracks, requiring some form of transport to get back to the start.

If you're not planning on staying overnight, walking any of the Great Walks is free, and the beginnings and ends of some of them are often completed as day trips (the Tongariro Crossing, for example, can be very popular in summer). The Department of Conservation, which ably manages the walks, sets a natural limit to visitor numbers; you will therefore need to book and pay in advance for overnight accommodation in the huts and tent sites. This money goes back towards the high cost of maintaining the huts and the tracks.

To cope with an ever-increasing demand from domestic and international tourists, a tenth Great Walk – the 55 kilometre Paparoa Track on the West Coast of the South Island – was recently added. Incorporating parts of the existing Croesus and Pororari tracks, a new section of track has been cut to link the others and two more huts have been built, allowing formed access to a previously difficult-to-reach part of New Zealand. Open to both walkers and cyclists all year round, the Paparoa is the first new track added since the Great Walks network was established back in 1993. There is the possibility of more tracks being raised to this status in the near future.

A BRIEF HISTORY

The first footsteps

Sometime between 800 and 1000 years ago, the ancestors of Māori set off from a place known as Hawaiki. They crossed the ocean in double-hulled waka (canoes), heading south into waters cooler than they had ever experienced before, searching for a new home. There was no way of knowing if some untouched southern land lay before them, or if it would be endless ocean. But they were committed.

After months at sea came the first sightings of land-based birds circling the sky, clumps of seaweed floating in the water, and finally a shroud of cloud gathering against the horizon. It is believed that no human had ever set foot on the shores these ancient travellers found, and they named the new country Aotearoa: Land of the Long White Cloud. Here, they would become tangata whenua – the people of the land.

Over time, different iwi (tribes) explored the North and South Islands by boat and on foot, discovering a coastline plump with seafood, rainforests lush with bird life, and a skyline pierced by ice-white mountains. Essentially, they made Aotearoa's first walking tracks as they travelled the country, foraging along sandy beaches but also finding routes through the forest, and even fixing wooden pegs as hand- and footholds so they could climb steep cliffs.

For the most part, Māori considered the mountain summits tapu (sacred), high places reserved for the gods and to be avoided when possible. Nonetheless, they made a number of first ascents – not for recreation, but out of need. According to oral tradition, the chief Tahurangi of the Taranaki iwi climbed Mt Taranaki, 'shining peak' (2518 m) – a clean-edged volcanic cone near the western coast of the North Island – as early as AD 1420 to lay claim to the land below. (The first European ascent wasn't until 1839.) The Ngāti Awa iwi buried some of their dead in a chasm atop the east peak of the green-cratered 280-metre Pūtauaki (Mt Edgecumbe), known as Te Tatau o te Rangi, 'the door of the sky'. And archaeological relics remain on the steep, tussock-covered ridges of the Tararua Range in the lower North Island.

In the Southern Alps and Fiordland, Māori explorers forged routes over mountain passes, along ridges and through valleys, searching for pounamu (greenstone), a type of jade used for weapons, tools and jewellery. Throughout Aotearoa, Māori created their own maps out of memory and terrain, naming features in songs and tales, tracing temporary charts on the ground, at times leaving ladders on cliffs and canoes at the sides of streams, or planting karaka trees to supply fruit for remote campsites. Nothing was written, yet the land flowed with the passage of people and stories.

European explorers

Dutch explorer Abel Tasman was about 90 kilometres off the west coast of the South Island when he saw a range of mountains hanging over the ocean. It was 13 December 1642, and Tasman recorded the sighting in his journal: 'Towards noon saw a large land, uplifted high.' One of the mountains that the explorer glimpsed on that day later became named after him – Mt Tasman is our second-highest peak.

Tasman is recognised as the first westerner to visit these shores, although it is still debated whether he actually set foot on land. A few days after making his historic sighting, he reached the top of the South Island, not far from what is now the Abel Tasman National Park. While his men came across local Māori (four of his men were in fact killed), he was loath to let his crew do any venturing inland. That fell to another northern hemisphere explorer.

Much later, in April 1773, on Captain James Cook's second voyage to New Zealand, the British naval sloop HMS *Resolution* was anchored in a sound crowded with small islands, in the south-western tip of what seemed like an untouched land. Like Māori hundreds of years before them, Captain Cook and his crew had been searching for an unknown realm – in their case, the giant blank on early maps that Europeans had hypothesised as Terra Incognita Australis, the 'Unknown Southern Land' (later found, of course, as Antarctica). After crossing the Antarctic Circle, they'd hunted, in vain, for a way south through the sea ice, until the coming winter drove them back toward warmer climates, their search unfulfilled.

Arriving on the coast of Fiordland on his second voyage, Cook would have been relieved that, for a while at least, they were free from the freezing, turbulent waters of the Tasman Sea and the frequent storms that swept up unbridled from the great Southern Ocean. They'd sailed into the inlet just as the sun's pale hue faded. And thus, Cook named the place Dusky Sound.

With the ship nestled in the sheltered lee of the islands, Cook allowed members of his crew to disembark and to try to ascend one of the many peaks rising sharply above a thickly forested shoreline. Early on 23 April – St George's Day – Richard Pickersgill, Joseph Gilbert and Anders Sparrman rowed ashore to Cascade Cove and started hiking up a curving, bush-covered spur. Fighting through dense undergrowth and sidling past a giant, iridescent waterfall, they finally clambered above the alpine scrub and followed an angling, craggy ridge. By mid-afternoon, nearly 1000 metres above the water, they had reached the apex.

Far below them, now, *Resolution* appeared becalmed, a dark splodge on the surface of the sound. From their high vantage point, the men had a sweeping view toward the vast, rugged interior of a place that would become known as Fiordland.

Hundreds of kilometres of seemingly uninhabited peaks and ridges, valleys and fiords, lakes and forests stretched to the horizon. This would likely have appeared to the men, and still appears so to many visitors today, as the wildest, most remote part of a wild, remote land.

From the late eighteenth century, more and more European sailors, missionaries, traders and explorers visited New Zealand, culminating in British colonisation. The Treaty of Waitangi, signed in 1840 between the British Crown and various Māori chiefs, was an attempt to formalise relations in this new outpost of the empire. Throughout the rest of the century there was extensive British settlement, and the introduction of a European economic and legal system led to most of New Zealand's land passing – legally, illegally, sometimes by brute force – from Māori to Pākehā (European New Zealander) ownership.

Enjoying and preserving the wild

While the early European explorers were often guided by Māori along their traditional tracks, the arrival of more settlers created a desire to hack road and rail routes into the interior of New Zealand. It took a major shift in thinking before people considered exploring the forested and mountainous regions as a recreational experience.

Recognising New Zealand's natural beauty was an important first step. In 1880, Donald Sutherland was the first European to discover the majestic Sutherland Falls near Milford Sound in Fiordland. A trail (later to become the Milford Track) was cut through the forests, and tourists visiting the sound were encouraged to walk the route and stay in huts. The track would colloquially become known as 'the finest walk in the world'.

The success of the Milford experience saw a demand for more walking tracks and huts in other regions of New Zealand, especially in the newly formed national parks of Tongariro and Te Papakura o Taranaki. Both domestic and international tourists came to realise that New Zealand was a prime destination for spectacular yet relatively comfortable, multi-day walking trips.

FLORA AND FAUNA

The native plants and animals, along with the varied landscapes, are a key element of New Zealand's unique natural beauty. Indeed, many New Zealanders identify so much with the land that being able to interact with our great outdoors has become an essential part of the national psyche. 'Getting away from it all' is a colloquialism well known among Kiwis. But what fauna and flora are now prevalent?

When the land mass that would become New Zealand separated from the supercontinent Gondwana about 85 million years ago through tectonic drift, it took with it a range of animals and plants that would later evolve in oceanic isolation, forming their own unique interrelationships. Over the centuries, other plants and animals arrived on wind or tide from neighbouring land masses, notably Australia, and made themselves at home here (one example is the pūkeko), but many of New Zealand's plants and animals are endemic: they occur nowhere else on the planet.

There were, and still are, two main forest types in New Zealand: beech and conifer–broadleaf. Beech is widespread, growing mainly in drier areas east of the mountains, as well as in colder and higher altitude regions. The four main varieties of beech make up nearly all of the South Island native forest but less than half of the North Island. (Incidentally, New Zealand beeches are unrelated to the northern hemisphere beech.) While beech forests can be quite open beneath the main canopy and are usually easy to travel through, conifer–broadleaf forests are more dense and lush, and generally enjoy wetter, warmer climates. And while a beech forest might

Pest control and eradication are an essential part of today's wildlife management.

be dominated by one or two species, conifer–broadleaf stands have a more varied canopy and undergrowth.

What is also interesting is that, while most of our trees are pollinated by birds and insects, beech seeds are spread by the wind or water and are thus slow to propagate over an area. Because of this there are areas known as 'beech gaps', where, despite a climate more suited to beech, conifer–broadleaf forests are more prevalent. Often these areas have been created by past glaciation or volcanic activity or naturally occurring fires. On the west coast of the South Island, despite the proximity of the mountains, there is a beech gap stretching some 500 kilometres.

During New Zealand's long period of isolation, the absence of any land-based mammals led to the evolution of unusual flightless birds, including the massive moa, the kiwi and the world's heaviest parrot, the kākāpō. These birds in some ways came to occupy the kinds of niches that, in other lands, would be taken by mammals. And at the same time, they had no need to develop defences against mammalian predators.

The very first human visitors would have encountered a land mostly covered in forest, rich in bird life (with perhaps 200 different species) as well as thousands of invertebrates. But the arrival of humans meant the loss of forests and the introduction of predators, such as stoats, cats and rats, that prey on our native animals, as well as other mammals (such as the possum) that devour our native plants. Collectively, this would lead to the loss of much of our natural habitat and the extinction of over half of the native bird species.

The onslaught by these introduced predators continues today, but conservationists are fighting back. It is thanks to individuals, such as Dr Geoffrey Orbell (who rediscovered the takahē in 1948) and Don Merton (who rescued the black robin from extinction), and to organisations, such as DOC (formerly the Wildlife Service) and the Royal Forest and Bird Protection Society, that so many of our native birds have survived.

Birds to watch out for

The Great Walks offer many chances to spot native birds, and if you are interested, a decent guide book would be a useful addition to your backpack. Here is a selection of particular birds to keep an eye out for on each walk:

WAIKAREMOANA: This heavily forested area is home to many bird species. One that might make itself known to you by chirping a complaint if you encroach on its territory is the whitehead. It is a small, almost fluffy-looking bird with, not surprisingly, a white head. Usually heard before they are seen, whiteheads often hang out in groups up in the tree canopy.

TONGARIRO: The pipit is unassuming in looks, similar to the common sparrow in colouring but thinner in the body and longer in the leg. But the pipit is particularly hardy. You might be battling through high winds and rain on the South Crater beneath mounts Ngāuruhoe and Tongariro, and choose to rest in the lee of a rock. There, looking as if nothing of note is occurring, a pipit may be ferreting around on the ground cover, searching for food.

WHANGANUI: The night-time call of the morepork, or ruru, is an eerie companion in the dark when you're camped on the edge of dense forest above the turbulence of the Whanganui River. This owl is a silent flier and hunter, and one of our few birds that fight back against some of the introduced predators, such as mice and rats. That said, it is still preyed upon by pests when nesting.

The weka is a common sight on parts of the Paparoa Track.

ABEL TASMAN: Since this is our only predominantly coastal Great Walk, it is appropriate to choose a seabird. The little blue penguin is quite shy, and tends to leave shore at dawn and return at dusk. Keep quiet and well hidden on one of the less populated beaches and you may be rewarded with a sighting, although you're more likely to see them off the coast as they tend to nest on the offshore islands there.

HEAPHY: The recent reintroduction of the takahē to the Gouland Downs area means that the Heaphy Great Walk has become even more special. The takahē is a large, flightless native bird with distinct blue-green plumage.

PAPAROA: You are very likely to meet the kleptomaniac weka during your walk on the Paparoa. This large, brown, flightless member of the rail family will likely even rummage through your pack if you let it. Don't, as it can run away surprisingly quickly if it finds something it fancies!

ROUTEBURN: There is an established population of the rare mohua (yellowhead), a small, insect-eating bird found in South Island and Stewart Island forests. Related to the whitehead, they are distinguishable by their obvious head colour, but you are unlikely to see them as they usually inhabit the upper canopy.

MILFORD: The kea is our only mountain parrot. Like the weka, it is mischievous and, given half a chance, also a bit of a thief. Kea are often heard before being seen, flying in the distance and calling out a longer version of their own name. Kea might act like they are starving, but please don't feed them because this only encourages bad habits and is contributing to a decline in numbers.

KEPLER: Traversing the alpine section, you may be lucky enough to see the endemic New Zealand falcon/kārearea. Much smaller than the introduced Australasian harrier, and very much rarer, it has a repetitive, shrill call, and can be highly aggressive if you get too close to its nest.

RAKIURA: The kākā is a large, forest-dwelling parrot and a cousin of the kea. It's often seen in flocks, flying noisily from tree to tree. But unlike the kea, which is restricted to the South Island, the kākā is found on all three main islands. Stewart Island is a great place to see them in the large numbers that used to exist over the rest of the country.

USING THIS BOOK

Tramping one of our Great Walks should be an engaging, wondrous, physically tiring and, hopefully, mostly stress-free experience. Likely you will be surprised at how easy it is to enter the rugged wilds surrounding you. While each of the walks is justifiably popular and well maintained, remember that you are entering an environment that contains all the vagaries of changing conditions and unpredictable weather. This book will help guide you through the decisions of what to do, when to go, what to take and, perhaps most importantly, what to be aware of. Each Great Walk has its own chapter packed with facts about what you might need, see and experience along the way, as well as maps and a track description to keep you on route. In each chapter, a section called Off the Track covers other things to do in each area.

PREPARATION

Being well prepared is a necessity for your own safety and enjoyment. If you are new to tramping (the Kiwi word for hiking and trekking), or even if you have some experience here or overseas, it is a good idea to start your Great Walk preparation well before you start your trip.

Clothing and equipment

You will need particular clothing and equipment to keep you safe and comfortable in the outdoors. Find a reputable shop to help with your kit-out. Bivouac Outdoor is a good choice in New Zealand, as it has a chain of shops in most major centres and each store carries a range of quality clothing, footwear and equipment. But there are also other suitable stores, and the key is to find a knowledgeable sales assistant who can provide you with decent advice, especially in terms of things like accurately sizing footwear and packs.

Having the appropriate clothing and equipment means a much more comfortable experience, and you will also be safer if the weather and/or track conditions deteriorate. Here's a list of what you might need.

Clothing

- First layers. Choose synthetics or wool for next-to-skin undergarments (including leggings and tee-shirts or long-sleeve shirts). Cotton has very poor insulating qualities and is a waste of weight. Synthetic products, such as polypropylene or other more expensive options, have a slightly better performance for weight when compared to wool, but wool doesn't hold your body odour anywhere near as much after a few days of sweating.

- Mid-layer tops. These can be a thicker version of the next-to-skin layer or a light fleece, and can be worn or removed depending on how hot or cold you become while walking each day.

- Insulation layer. A down or synthetic jacket or a heavy fleece is needed for those cool morning starts and again at the end of the day after the sun sets.

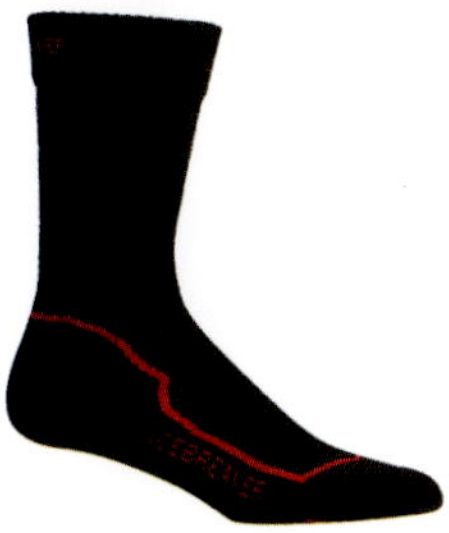

- Leggings. Both a pair of shorts and longs (lightweight nylon, rather than cotton or jeans) will come in useful. If it's cold you can wear your next-to-skin leggings underneath.

- Socks, hat and gloves. Cheaper socks are more likely to give you blisters. Both a beanie for warmth and a sun hat to help protect against sunburn are advisable.

- Rainwear. You might get away without waterproof over-trousers (though if the forecast is for rain you will be more comfortable with some), but a bombproof raincoat is a must. Don't get a cheap one – you may come to regret it!

- Footwear. Buy a decent pair of lightweight boots (shoes will be enough for the Abel Tasman), and get a knowledgeable store assistant to help size them. Don't rush this purchase if you want to be able to walk comfortably. As a rule you don't want to buy active footwear that's too snug, because your feet will likely swell up during activity.

- Other clothing items worth carrying include a neck gaiter or buff, and comfortable sunglasses. Note that you do not need to carry lots of extra clothing items. Rather, consider having just one extra set of tops, bottoms and socks (so you always have dry clothes to wear at the end of each day).

Equipment

- Pack (rucksack). A pack between 40 and 60 litres (depending on how efficient you are with your clothing and equipment) should be more than enough for most of the Great Walks. If you are finding that it's too small, perhaps you are carrying too much stuff. Again, ask a store assistant to help choose and fit one properly to your body shape. Be sure to bring a pack liner to keep your gear dry if it rains; a big, heavy-duty plastic bag will do the job.

- Sleeping bag. A down sleeping bag will be warmer and pack down smaller than a synthetic bag of the same weight, but will also likely be more expensive. A silk liner (like an enclosed sheet to sleep in inside the bag) will keep the bag from getting too 'manky' from your day of exercise. Also, be sure to purchase a good dry-bag to store your sleeping bag in during the trip.

- Tent. Modern nylon tents are lightweight, but some designs can be fiddly to put up. Have a go at pitching it in the shop before you commit to a particular model.

- Personal locator beacon (PLB). These days there is no excuse for not carrying a beacon. They are lightweight and relatively inexpensive to buy or hire, and can be a lifesaver if you get hurt or lost. Please be sure to only activate it in a genuine emergency.

- First-aid kit. A basic kit is all you will require, but include insect-repellent, sunscreen, something to cover and pad blisters, and plenty of tape (which can also be used to repair broken boots and packs if needed).

- Stove. While cooking facilities are usually provided in the huts, if you are camping you will need a stove. There are plenty of small, lightweight

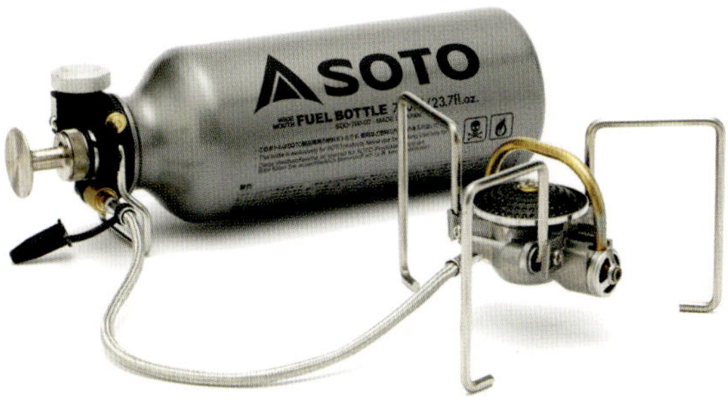

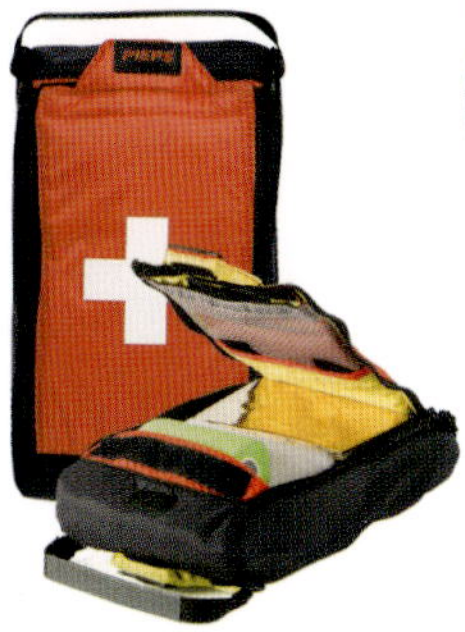

options. Butane/propane gas stoves are much easier to operate than ones requiring petrol or spirits. Make sure your billy (cooking pot) fits easily on top and has a lid.

- Walking poles. One is usually enough, but some people prefer to use two.
- Cup, plate, spoon, pocket knife, lighter or matches.
- A range of small dry-bags for ease of sorting and storage.
- Food. This is down to personal preference, but freeze-dried meals for dinner (just add boiling water) are easy and filling. Having a range of small snacking options during the day is a good idea, as well as an emergency supply in case your walk takes longer.
- Water bottle. Occasionally, some sections of tracks run out of water, especially in summer. Check with DOC beforehand about whether you will need to carry extra water (or water purifiers), and make sure you have enough water containers for this.

- Map. While the track you are doing should be well marked and obvious, it is still a good idea to purchase a map of the area. Along with reaffirming where you are and where you are heading, it usually includes a lot of extra and interesting information. If you don't know how to read a map, find someone to teach you.

WHICH TRACK TO DO

If this is your first Great Walk and you are not particularly experienced at tramping, perhaps choose an easier track like the Abel Tasman. There are no big hill climbs and the terrain will let you test your fitness and finetune your outdoor skills before you try one of the more mountainous tracks. The Abel Tasman is also child-friendly, with lots of camping choices spaced all the way along the track.

Fitness

For the uninitiated, carrying a heavy pack (especially uphill) can be physically draining. If possible, do some training in the hills around home (yes, wearing a fully laden pack) before you venture on to the track. If there are no hills nearby, any form of aerobic training that uses your legs and core is worthwhile. Even an elevated walking machine at a gym will help; you might get funny looks from the other gym users if you are wearing a pack, but it's worth it. Being fitter and stronger will make your Great Walk experience that much more manageable and enjoyable.

Skill level

Although the Great Walks are well maintained and have lots of facilities, learning the correct skills for travelling in the outdoors is still a good idea. Things like pitching a tent, reading a map, lighting a cooker, dealing with (or, better yet, preventing) blisters, managing more serious first-aid situations, and understanding the changes in weather in the mountains are fundamental to a safe trip in the back country. See if there is a walking or tramping club nearby to where you live and enquire if it runs basic outdoor courses. Find out if any of your family or friends are experienced trampers and, if so, get them to show you what they have learnt. Staying safe in the outdoors should always be your main priority.

Season

Some of the Great Walks are open only during certain times of the year, usually because of the threat of avalanches in the higher mountain sections. Other tracks are open all year round and, while colder during the winter months, they are likely to be less crowded. The weather in New Zealand is very changeable and sometimes quite unpredictable (see more in the Weather section on page 25), and you may experience poor conditions during any time of the year. Check the DOC website (www.doc.govt.nz) for updates, such as whether the open season for a particular walk has changed.

Booking

You will need to book your bed or campsite online with DOC well before you decide to do the trip. The online process is easy, but don't delay: some of the Great Walks become booked out very quickly, especially during the more popular summer months.

This is also a good time to consider what transport you will require getting to and from each end of the track (the chapters on each of the Great Walks will spell out any transport requirements and options). You may need to book this well in advance also.

JUST PRIOR TO YOUR TRIP

There are a number of things you should do and check on just before you start your Great Walk.

Not all of the Great Walks are as smooth or easy as this section of the Kepler Track.

Check track conditions

It is important to check with DOC just before you begin your trip to get updated conditions on the track. Some of the Great Walks are exposed to snowfall and avalanche risk at various times of the year. They might be closed, or detours (such as a costly helicopter ride) may be in place. Also there may be a flooding risk depending on the weather, or landslips that are blocking the track.

Sign in online

Immediately before you start your walk you should fill out your trip intentions on the Adventure Smart website (www.adventuresmart.org.nz), and then forward the information to a trusted contact who is not on your journey but who can raise the alarm with authorities if you fail to return on time. It is important to ensure your trusted contact has received this information and understands what is required of them (your safety may depend on it), and that you contact them again as soon as you have completed your trip.

Weather

The weather in New Zealand can be changeable and unpredictable. While there is a general pattern to the high- and low-pressure systems that cross our narrow islands and dictate our prevailing weather, these can alter course from the forecast or intensify at short notice. This can work two ways: sometimes the weather is better than predicted (which is great), but sometimes an unexpected downpour of rain can raise river levels, or higher winds can make alpine pass crossings more challenging and even dangerous. Be sure to check www.metservice.com and www.metvuw.com for updated forecasts before you start your trip (Metservice has a section on weather in the national parks). While you should also check with DOC (call the centre closest to your track) about the predicted conditions, it is a good idea to familiarise yourself with our weather and forecasting.

DURING YOUR TRIP

These things are important in terms of safety and comfort during each day of your journey.

Communication

There may be a DOC hut warden at each of the huts you stay at (or close to your campsites) during your Great Walk. They are great sources of information about what to expect on the track ahead and what the weather holds in store. But they are not there to keep track of your personal progress. It is a good idea to fill out the hut books each night so that, in an emergency and in case you get lost, the rescue services have a written trail to follow. Note that there is unlikely to be any cellphone coverage on the track, but you should have a personal locator beacon (PLB) with you, in case of emergency.

There are various obstacles to overcome on the Great Walks – like this swing bridge on the Heaphy Track.

In an emergency

If by chance you have cellphone coverage (this is very unlikely on most of the Great Walks) call 111 (be sure, if you can, to have an accurate description of your location). Otherwise, activate your PLB, apply first aid if required to any victims, move to a safe and sheltered place if you can, and wait for help.

Health and personal safety

- Be sure to drink from reliable water sources. There might be DOC signs advising what is safe to drink, and it may be a good idea to have some form of purifying system. (Tablets are the cheapest option, but ask at an outdoors store.)

- Hypothermia (getting too cold) can lead to death in extreme cases. Manage your clothing layers appropriately. Look out for early signs of hypothermia; if you don't know what these are, perhaps doing a basic first-aid course is a good idea before your trip.

- Be sure to keep covered with clothing and sunscreen to avoid getting sunburnt.

- Sandflies (these very friendly insects deserve their own explanation later), wasps and various other small flying bugs can and do sting or bite.

- It is a good idea to manage your general energy levels with food, and take rests when you need them. Completing these walks is not a race. Take your time and enjoy your surroundings.

Sandflies

New Zealand is mostly free of dangerous animals in the wild, but we do have a number of pests, and it is perhaps the pesky sandfly that will leave the biggest impression on those enjoying the Great Walks. Sandflies will be found in most back-country regions under around 1000 metres, and are more prevalent when it is warm and wet. These wee bloodsuckers have been nicknamed many things over the years, none of them complimentary.

They are especially feisty on the lower, western half of the South Island and nowhere more so than Fiordland. Insect-repellent is a must, the stronger the better!

Natural hazards

While you are unlikely to experience an earthquake during your time on a Great Walk, it is still a possibility (and an even smaller possibility that it might be a big one). There's a remote risk, too, of volcanic eruptions in the North Island. Find out beforehand what you should do during a shake, and consider this another good reason to follow the communication recommendations listed earlier. Other natural hazards to consider include the risk of avalanches, especially in winter and spring and the risk of flooding.

Looking after your stuff

Anywhere there are people theft can be a risk, and New Zealand is no different. While physical violence is very unlikely, someone breaking into your unattended vehicle parked at the end of a track is more of a possibility. Take valuables with you or, better yet, leave them somewhere safe rather than in the car.

Driving

If you're unfamiliar with New Zealand roads and driving conditions, they can be challenging. Big open stretches may tempt you to floor the pedal, but our roads can be surprisingly narrow and curvy, so watch your speed. Kiwi drivers are known for being a little impatient at times, too, and slow driving can create just as much risk in some instances. If you have a queue behind you, pull over to let the other vehicles past. Pay attention to the road, rather than the scenery. And keep left!

Tramping responsibilities

These are a series of guidelines and expectations for travelling in the outdoors. Some focus on protecting the environment, others on being courteous to fellow trampers.

It is important to consider others when places are busy – like the Mintaro Hut on the Milford Track.

- Be self-sufficient if you can. If something goes wrong, don't count on a rescue team turning up immediately. Stay calm and make good decisions.
- Minimise the amount of resources you use. Take less packaging; purify water rather than buying bottled water; avoid using firewood in a hut unless necessary, but replenish any wood or kindling you do use, and only use the wood supplied rather than breaking off branches from live trees.
- Camp in designated areas.
- Pay your hut fees.
- Share hut space, and keep huts tidy.
- Take all of your rubbish with you and pick up any rubbish you find.
- Leave hut food if it is not yours, unless it has clearly been marked as free for anyone to use.
- Report any damage you cause or see to DOC.
- Stick to the marked track to prevent further erosion and vegetation damage. This will help keep you safe, too: in mist, fog or rain, it's easy to become disoriented and wander into potentially dangerous terrain.
- As a rule keep to the left on the track if it is busy, and let people pass if they are moving more quickly than you.
- Manage toilet waste. Use toilets provided (there are plenty on all of the Great Walks), otherwise take a trowel and bury your waste at least 50 metres from waterways.
- Don't wash in streams.
- Take only photos and leave only footprints. Take nothing from the environment – no souvenirs.

- Do not disturb or feed wildlife.
- Keep boots and equipment clean to prevent the spread of unwanted organisms.
- Do not take your dog into national parks.
- Do not light fires. Use a cooking stove if needed, and be very aware of fire restrictions.
- Didymo, or 'rock snot', is an alga that invades and chokes waterways. It can be spread by careless trampers. Check, clean and dry your gear.
- Finally, learn about the environment and its unique attributes so you are aware of how to protect it and why it is worth protecting.

Nikau palms add an exotic feel to the West Coast portion of the Heaphy Track.

LAKE WAIKAREMOANA

SEA OF RIPPLING WATERS

View over Lake Waikaremoana on the first day.

LAKE WAIKAREMOANA

SEA OF RIPPLING WATERS // 46 KM, 3–4 DAYS

— HIGHLIGHTS

- Take in the view from Panekiri Bluff.
- Walk beneath ancient trees.
- Swim in the lake.
- Identify as many different native birds as you can.
- Consider the history of the landscape and its people.

IMAGINE AN ANCIENT, remote, rugged landscape. Consider, that to many, this landscape holds a deeply spiritual significance, not just to those who live nearby but to the entire nation.

The local people – Ngāi Tūhoe, the 'children of the mist' – have resided in Te Urewera for centuries, and they remain passionate guardians. Their connection to the land, along with its geographical isolation, has played a large part in ensuring farming, forestry and other invasive developments remain largely discouraged. Te Urewera is indeed a living treasure.

Lake Waikaremoana sits as the beating heart of Te Urewera, its lifeblood flowing through the rivers and streams that merge into and run out of the lake. It feels appropriate to begin the overall journey of New Zealand's Great Walks here. The history of this place is filled with legends and stories, all woven into the fabric of the landscape. To understand such a history is to recognise the many challenges that have faced the land we call Aotearoa.

Covering an area of approximately 2130 square kilometres, Te Urewera is (or, more accurately, was) the largest of the North Island's four national parks. Due mostly to its remoteness, especially when compared to other areas of the North Island, the region was one of the last in New Zealand to be claimed by the British during colonisation in the nineteenth century. But Tūhoe never recognised the new sovereignty.

N
to Murupara
TE UREWERA
HUIARAU RANGE
Hopuruahine Strm
Hopuruahine
Hopuruahine Landing
Whanganui
Lake Waikareiti
Tapuaenui
Whanganui Inlet
Waiharuru
Aniwaniwa
PUKETUKUTUKU PENINSULA
Marauiti
Maraunui
Lake Waikaremoana
Wairaomoana (Wairau Arm)
Panekiri Bluff
Korokoro
Korokoro Falls
PANEKIRI RANGE
Onepoto
Waiopaoa
Puketapu
Panekire
Waiopaoa Strm
Waikaretaheke River
38
to Wairoa
0
5
10 km

In 1957 the land known as Te Urewera was declared a national park by the Crown. But then, in 2013, in a bid to settle ongoing grievances with Tūhoe, representatives from the New Zealand government signed a deal with the iwi (tribe). As part of the negotiations, Tūhoe gained more control over its ancestral land. Under the Te Urewera Act 2014 the area ceased to be recognised as a national park. Instead, it became the same legal entity as a person, its management now administered by the Te Urewera Board (with representation from both Tūhoe and the Crown).

With the land still open to the public, the Department of Conservation has continued maintaining the tracks and facilities in conjunction with the Board. So it is with extra significance that visitors are given permission to walk the Lake Waikaremoana track, most of which follows the shoreline of the lake. Tramp here also in the knowledge you have entered the largest remaining area of native forest in the North Island.

Usually taking 3 to 4 days to complete, the track passes through a range of landscapes including rainforest, wetlands and a magical-feeling 'goblin forest' on the flanks of Panekiri Bluff. Te Urewera is home to nearly every species of North Island native forest bird, providing visitors with a glimpse of the bird life that once flourished throughout New Zealand. The melodic call of tūī will likely follow you everywhere, along with the high-pitched trill of inquisitive whiteheads and the heavy wing-beats of kererū

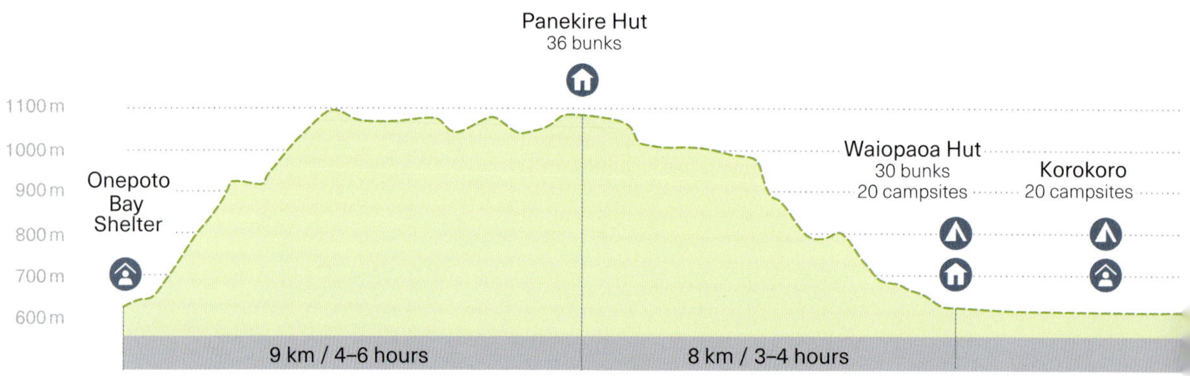

Occasional glimpses of the lake during the ascent from Onepoto Shelter to Panekire Hut.

(native pigeon) flying past. And at night, listen for the calls of the kiwi, our national bird.

This is a special, significant region, and one that has had its guardianship rightfully returned to the local tangata whenua (people of the land).

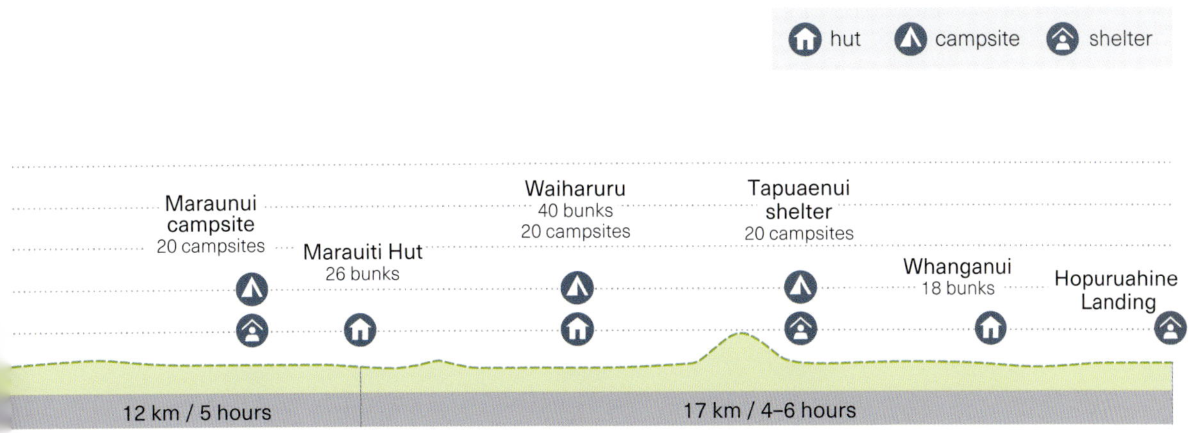

The lookout rock at Panekiri Bluff.

TRACK DETAILS

LOCATION: Te Urewera, northern Hawke's Bay
TRACK TYPE: This is a semicircular route that can be walked in either direction, but transport will be needed at the northern and/or southern end of the track. Access points are at Onepoto Bay and Hopuruahine Landing. The track is easy to follow but there are sections that are steep, rough and slippery underfoot, especially when compared to some of the other Great Walks. A walking pole and sturdy footwear are recommended.

START POINT: Onepoto Bay Shelter
END POINT: Hopuruahine Landing
DISTANCE: 46 km
TIME: 3–4 days
SEASON: This track is open all year round, and huts and campsites will need to be booked in advance.

GRADING: There is only one really big hill on the track, which is a 600 metre climb taking you up to around 1100 metres above sea level, and it is dealt with on the first day. The rest of the walk is mostly undulating and easy. Overall, moderate fitness is required.
DOC HUTS: Panekire (36 bunks), Waiopaoa (30 bunks), Marauiti (26 bunks), Waiharuru (40 bunks), Whanganui (18 bunks)
DOC CAMPSITES: Waiopaoa (20 sites), Korokoro (20 sites), Maraunui (20 sites), Waiharuru (20 sites), Tapuaenui (20 sites)

RECOMMENDED TRIP OPTION: Leave your car (if you have one) at the nearby DOC visitor centre and campsite at Aniwaniwa, and arrange a short vehicle ride to Onepoto Shelter. Plan to stay at Panekire, Waiopaoa and Waiharuru huts, and then have a prearranged boat pick-up at Hopuruahine Landing (or somewhere nearby), which will take you back to your vehicle.

PLANNING

ACCESS: Lake Waikaremoana can be approached from two directions. State Highway 38 is the only road that leads through Te Urewera, and it is winding and unsealed for around 90 kilometres. This road links Wairoa on the east coast with Murupara in the central North Island, and it passes right by the lake and the DOC visitor centre and campsite at Aniwaniwa. If you are travelling by public transport, there is a locally arranged shuttle from Wairoa, which can take you to the lake.

Once at the lake, you can find privately owned shuttle buses and water taxis that provide transport from Aniwaniwa to either end of the track. This allows you to leave your vehicle securely at the DOC visitor centre.

ACCOMMODATION, FOOD AND EQUIPMENT: The nearest cities are Napier and Gisborne, and these are the best places to get tramping equipment and food, although there is a decent supermarket at Wairoa. Wairoa also has plenty of accommodation options before the drive in to Waikaremoana. The lakeside Waikaremoana Holiday Park (also the site of the DOC visitor centre) is the best accommodation close to the track, and it also has some food for sale.

Some of the track is
rough underfoot.

Panekire Hut has a great view over the lake.

WEATHER: This part of the North Island can get plenty of rain, so be sure to take a decent raincoat and warm clothes. The first day also climbs to around 1000 metres, so be prepared for the possibility of cold temperatures. But, in summer especially, this area can also get very dry and hot, so make sure you carry enough water for sections of the track where there isn't a local water source (the first day in particular).

TRACK CONDITIONS: Parts of the track, notably on the first day, are not as well formed as those you'll find on some of the other Great Walks. Tree roots especially may be slippery, so take care underfoot. Generally, though, most of the track is in good condition.

TRACK DESCRIPTION

Onepoto Shelter to Panekire Hut: 3–5 hrs, 9 km

The start of the track, climbing through forest up the edge of the Panekiri Range, is quite steep, rough, and slippery with tree roots. It is slow going at first, but that's okay because the gradient will encourage you to take lots of rests and appreciate the environment.

The ascent through the forest is constant – some might say relentless – but there are occasional clearings to look out over the lake and see how much height you have gained. This is the most strenuous part of the trip, but the views from the Panekiri lookout more than make up for it.

Stop for the obligatory selfie at the lookout, before continuing through moss-covered beech trees – forming the aptly named 'goblin forest' – that have grown in knobbled and deformed ways due to the wind on this exposed part of the track. The high point, Puketapu Trig, is at 1180 metres, and soon after you will reach the spectacularly situated Panekire Hut.

Note that, in summer especially, the water tank at Panekire Hut can get low (the DOC visitor centre may know if you need to carry extra water).

Panekire Hut to Waiopaoa Hut: 3–4 hrs, 7.5 km

This is not a long day, but it gives you plenty of time to take in the ambience of the forest and, later, relax by the lake.

From the hut the track continues along the ridge before making a steep descent back to the lake. The forest here is as impressive as any on the other Great Walks. Sleeping giants of rimu, beech and kāmahi form the canopy, while beneath them younger trees compete for space, and the ground either side of the track is carpeted with ferns (including ponga or silver tree fern), grasses and saplings.

You will be accompanied by birdsong in the branches overhead, and possibly by a number of different species with an eye on you, some of them inquisitive and others unobtrusive. Keep a lookout for warblers, creepers, whiteheads, riflemen, tomtits and fantails. New Zealand may not have many big, flashy birds, but our smaller feathery friends more than make up for it with their subtle quirks and habits. Whiteheads can be quite nosy and boisterous at your invasion of their space, while the mouselike riflemen seem to scuttle about on trunks and branches.

Back at lake level and near the mouth of the Waiopaoa Inlet is the Waiopaoa hut and campsite. Brave the cool water and feisty local swans for a refreshing dip, and enjoy watching the evening light seep from the surface of the lake.

Waiopaoa Hut to Waiharuru Hut: 5–6 hrs, 17.5 km

From here most of the track follows along the lake edge, with only short detours around various hills and other landforms. Although today's distance might seem a long one, the travel is generally easy.

Leaving Waiopaoa Hut, walk up the Waiopaoa Stream for a relatively short distance before traversing to grassy flats and then returning to the sanctuary of more forest. As you walk, perhaps consider the aptly named children of the mist who have long lived here, walking their own secret trails through the forest.

There is the option of a short side trip to Korokoro Falls just before you reach the Korokoro suspension bridge. The falls are quite impressive and only half an hour from the turn-off.

Carrying along the main track, you will soon come to the Korokoro Campsite and then Maraunui Campsite after another 2 hours. Marauiti Hut is only 30 minutes past the Maraunui Campsite. Spend the night here or, for a longer day's walking, continue another 2 hours to the more commodious Waiharuru Hut and nearby campsite.

Waiharuru Hut to Hopuruahine Landing: 3–4 hrs, 13 km

The track follows the lakeshore, then rises over the neck of the Puketukutuku Peninsula, before descending to the Tapuaenui Campsite on the Whanganui arm of the lake. From here the track follows the shore again, eventually reaching Whanganui Hut, which is set in a clearing beside the Whanganui Stream. This is a relaxing place to stop for lunch.

From Whanganui Hut, the track reaches the usual water taxi pick-up and drop-off point after approximately 45 minutes (be clear with your transport operator about where you are being picked up). To continue further, follow

Most of the walk weaves through thick forest.

Waiopaoa Hut is close to the shoreline of the lake.

the track along grassy flats alongside Hopuruahine River to reach the Hopuruahine suspension bridge and another landing.

Warning: There is the potential for rock fall at the Hereheretaua Bridge. Please pass through this area quickly, especially during and shortly after rainfall.

POINTS OF INTEREST

Children of the mist

As touched on in the introduction to this chapter, there is a special and lasting bond between Te Urewera and Tūhoe. The iwi takes its name from Tūhoe-pōtiki, a great-grandson of the chieftain Toroa. It is said that Tūhoe fought his brothers over the local land and its resources and won. Te Urewera is steep country, mostly heavily forested and with fast-flowing rivers, and the Tūhoe people lived in the river valleys and the few forest clearings that existed. As there was little land that could be easily farmed, the people depended on the forest for everything, from shelter to food and clothing.

The arrival of Pākehā (European New Zealanders) wrought huge changes on New Zealand and on the tangata whenua, but the remoteness of Te Urewera meant that contact between Tūhoe and Europeans came much later than it did for other tribes. Tūhoe's first major brush with Pākehā came during the wars of the 1860s, in which the iwi was wrongly accused of rebelling against the Crown when a missionary was killed in Ōpōtiki. During the fighting, the Crown seized the iwi's most usable land. Worse was to come when government troops again invaded Te Urewera, this time in search of the resistance leader Te Kooti Arikirangi Te Turuki. Te Kooti had launched a campaign against the government in Poverty Bay in 1868, and Tūhoe sheltered and supported him.

Today, many Tūhoe still live and hunt for food in Te Urewera, and the iwi's spiritual and cultural traditions have rightly retained close links with the forested hills. While enjoying the Great Walk, do so in the knowledge that this area has many pockets of private land, some held sacred by Tūhoe. In places where the track crosses private land, you are welcome to pass through, but it is important, and respectful, to stay on the marked track.

A land in motion

New Zealand sits astride the actively shifting Indo-Australian and Pacific tectonic plates. Measured by earthquakes, occasional volcanic eruptions and landslides, their movement translates to a landscape forever in motion. The common boundary of the two plates runs beneath Te Urewera; it pushed a bedrock of siltstone, mudstone and sandstone up from the ocean floor about two million years ago, and still creates tectonic uplift today. But while the land itself is geologically old, the waters of Lake Waikaremoana are considered to be relatively young. When a huge landslip choked a part of the Waikaretaheke River about 2200 years ago, flowing water built up behind it, over time creating a lake around 250 metres at its deepest point.

Local flora and fauna

On arriving at Te Urewera, you'll be impressed at how extensively ancient trees still cover the landscape. Much of this land has remained mostly untouched, other than the few marked and unmarked trails passing through it. And while introduced animals such as possums and deer (both now recognised as pests) have impacted the flora, the resilience of the more than 600 native plant species has helped preserve the land's aura.

Along with the impressive vegetation, there is a wide range of birds living and thriving in the forest. As well as the ones already mentioned, there are the noisy kākā (forest parrot), the colourful kākāriki (parakeet), the inquisitive North Island robin, and the feisty New Zealand falcon. Both of New Zealand's very rare and very small native bat species, the long-tailed and the short-tailed, live in the park, and if you're lucky you may see them flying around after dark in the clearings near some of the huts.

Saving the kiwi

Prior to people arriving in New Zealand, there could have been as many as 12 million kiwi here. Following the human introduction of rats, stoats, ferrets, weasels, dogs, cats, pigs and possums, the bird's population plummeted and is now only a tiny fraction of the original number.

Recently, DOC and the Lake Waikaremoana Hapū Restoration Trust formed a partnership to halt the continually dropping numbers of kiwi at Waikaremoana, with predator control on the Puketukutuku Peninsula becoming the main focus. Traps have been laid to kill stoats, possums and rats, and local kiwi numbers monitored to measure the result. Since the trapping programme started, kiwi numbers have steadily increased in the area, and visitors are now more likely to hear their calls at night.

OFF THE TRACK

Tramp the Manuoha–Waikareiti Track

Starting from near the end of the Lake Waikaremoana Great Walk, the Manuoha–Waikareiti Track is a spectacular and challenging hike suited to experienced trampers. Considered an advanced track, the 32 kilometre trail takes a minimum of 3 days to complete and there are two huts en route where you can spend the night. The first hut, Manuoha, is set on top

The track continues around the edge of the lake, beneath ancient trees.

of Mt Manuoha, which, at 1392 metres, is the highest point in Te Urewera. It sleeps six people and does not need to be pre-booked. The second, Sandy Bay, is more modern, with bunks for 18 people, and you'll need to book in advance.

Note that parts of this track are little more than a marked route and so require more advanced back-country skills and route-finding ability than on a Great Walk. For more information on the track, and for updated conditions, check with the local DOC visitor centre at Aniwaniwa.

Drive the East Cape

It's a long, winding drive up the coast from Napier, past Gisborne, and into the heart of the East Cape. The main highway is not in particularly good shape. Slumps in the land have buckled the road in many places, a reminder of both the high rainfall and history of the land. The establishment of early Pākehā settlements saw a once heavily forested region clear-felled or burnt for grazing.

Lake Waikaremoana is a constant presence.

North of Gisborne, communities are few and far between. Gravel roads pierce the rugged interior of the upper East Cape, but just one sealed road circumnavigates it, keeping close to the coast for much of the journey from Gisborne to Ōpōtiki. Despite tourists and locals travelling this route, the road still has a remote and lonely feel to it, and the drive is recommended as a way of getting off the beaten path of busier parts of New Zealand.

Climb Mt Hikurangi

Hikurangi, near Ruatoria on the East Cape, is the highest non-volcanic mountain in the North Island, and fifth-highest overall. At 1754 metres, it dominates the north-eastern fringe of the Raukumara Forest Park, 115,000 hectares of dense bush and steep-sided hills. It is also the first

place in mainland New Zealand – and indeed, thanks to the location of the international dateline, the world – to see the sun.

Just as Te Urewera is significant to Tūhoe, so too are Hikurangi and Raukumara to Ngāti Porou. Hikurangi is their maunga – their mountain of significance, of identity, of strength. It is respectful to gain permission from local Ngāti Porou representatives in Ruatoria before attempting to climb the mountain. The effort, and the views, are certainly worth it. There is a hut on the flanks of Hikurangi if you would prefer to stay the night, and thus have a greater chance to see the sun rising from the summit. There is a track to follow above the hut, and the final stretch to the summit is exposed and a bit of a scramble. Note also that the upper slopes of the mountain can be covered with snow in winter and, if so, you will need an ice axe and crampons.

The expanse between
Mt Ngāuruhoe and Mt Ruapehu.

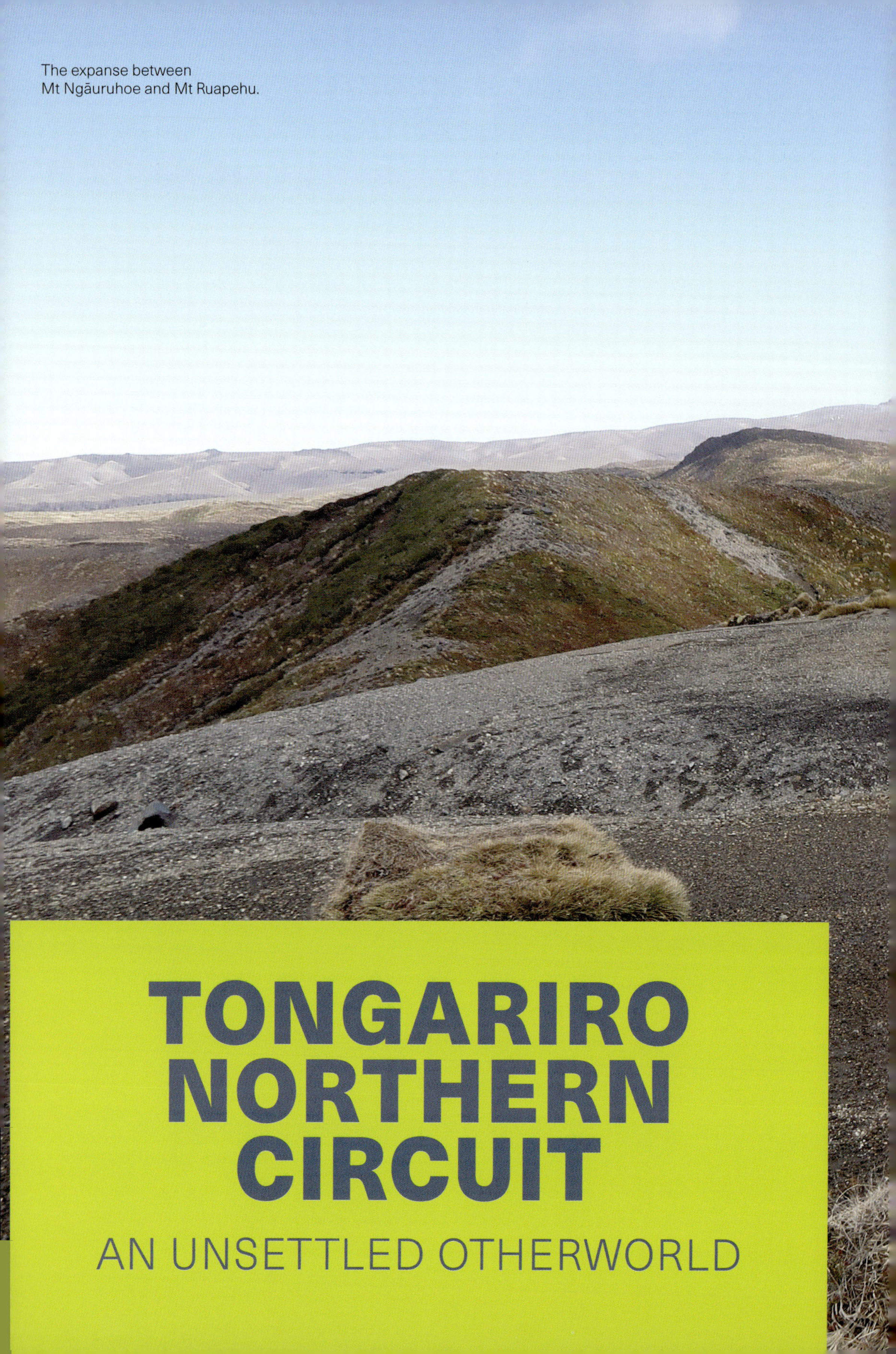

TONGARIRO NORTHERN CIRCUIT

AN UNSETTLED OTHERWORLD

TONGARIRO NORTHERN CIRCUIT

AN UNSETTLED OTHERWORLD // 43 KM, 2–4 DAYS

— HIGHLIGHTS

- Walk past an active volcano.
- Peer into a volcanic crater.
- See the vividly blue Emerald Lakes.
- Experience a landscape of many and surprising contrasts.
- Take in views across the Central North Island.

THE ELEVATED CUSP of the Central North Island is an unexpectedly varied landscape. Dominated by the Volcanic Plateau, the land is part desert, part alpine (with three volcanic mountains), part open grasslands and part dense forest. This is a land of contrasts and surprises. What at first glance appears to be rather harsh, dry and barren turns out on closer inspection to have many interesting aspects, with a large portion of the area coming under the protective banner of the Tongariro National Park.

To the west of the three great volcanoes lie the ancient podocarp forests, while to the east the dramatic Rangipō Desert stretches to the aptly named Desert Road. Between are hills of old lava flows and other volcanic debris – some covered with alpine grasses, flax and stunted hebes, and others bare of foliage and windblown. This land is lashed by rain, baked by the sun's heat, smothered in snow and sometimes even overwhelmed by volcanic eruptions.

And then there are the mountains themselves: Tongariro (1961 m), Ngāuruhoe (2287 m) and, forming the highest point in the North Island, Ruapehu (2797 m). Along with New Zealand's other volcanic zones, they form the southern end of what is known as the Pacific Ring of Fire, a volcanic chain that extends through the Solomon Islands, Indonesia, Japan and the west coast of the American continent. This huge arc of volcanoes is the result of friction between the underlying tectonic plates, and our three central volcanoes are renowned for still being particularly active.

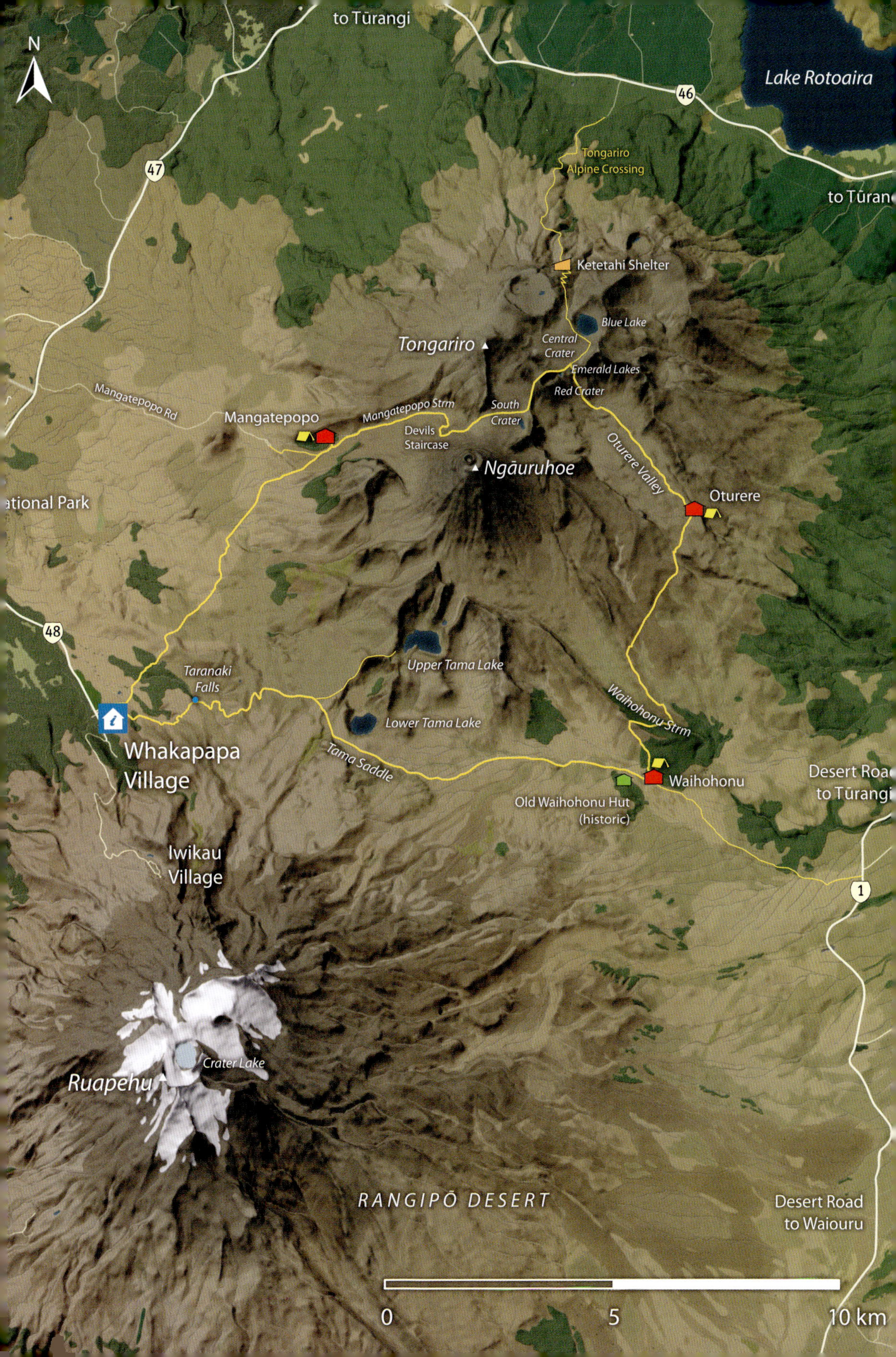

N
to Tūrangi
Lake Rotoaira
46
47
Tongariro Alpine Crossing
to Tūran
Ketetahi Shelter
Blue Lake
Tongariro
Central Crater
Emerald Lakes
Red Crater
Mangatepopo Rd
Mangatepopo
Mangatepopo Strm
South Crater
Devils Staircase
Ngāuruhoe
Oturere Valley
Oturere
ational Park
48
Taranaki Falls
Upper Tama Lake
Lower Tama Lake
Waihohonu Strm
Whakapapa Village
Tama Saddle
Waihohonu
Desert Roa to Tūrangi
Old Waihohonu Hut (historic)
Iwikau Village
1
Crater Lake
Ruapehu
RANGIPŌ DESERT
Desert Road to Waiouru
0
5
10 km

The Tongariro Northern Circuit winds its way around and partway over Tongariro and Ngāuruhoe, and then beneath the summit of Ruapehu. Showcasing spectacular volcanic terrain littered with scoria, pumice and other debris from old eruptions, this Great Walk passes close to active craters and vividly blue alpine lakes. It traverses old glacial valleys and crosses exposed plains with little vegetation to soften or shelter.

Experiencing and understanding this land is to appreciate that it is constantly moving, always restless. In places fragile and prone to erosion, it exists because of previous eruptions as well as high levels of snow and rainfall. Perhaps what is most striking about walking the Tongariro Northern Circuit is that, at times, you may feel as though you are moving through a moonscape rather than somewhere supposedly based on Earth. This is indeed an unsettled otherworld.

TRACK DETAILS

LOCATION: Tongariro National Park (Central North Island)
TRACK TYPE: This is a circular route that can be walked in either direction and with a number of possible access points. The track is well marked and signposted, but some sections are steep, rough, and/or slippery underfoot. A walking pole and sturdy footwear are strongly recommended.

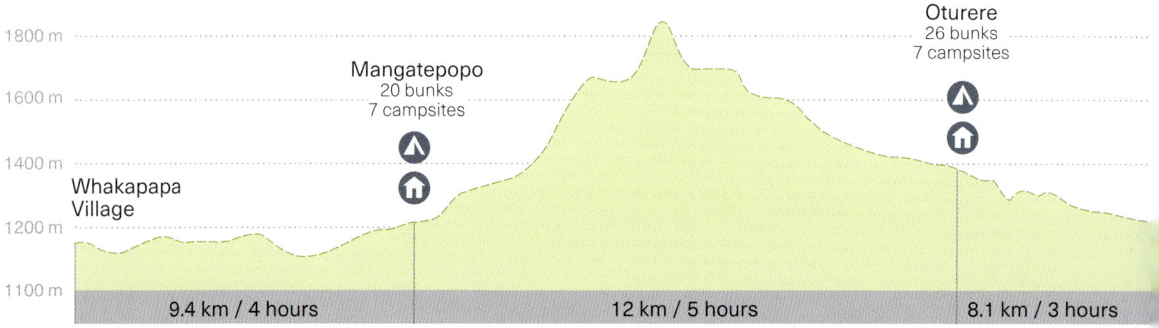

START POINT: Whakapapa Village
END POINT: Whakapapa Village
DISTANCE: 43 km
TIME: 2–4 days
SEASON: 21 October – 30 April. This track is to be completed *only* during the open season unless you have specific winter mountaineering equipment and knowledge. In winter the higher sections especially, and sometimes all of the track, can become covered in snow.
GRADING: Moderate fitness required
DOC HUTS: Mangatepopo (20 bunks), Oturere (26 bunks), Waihohonu (28 bunks)
DOC CAMPSITES: Mangatepopo (7 sites), Oturere (7 sites), Waihohonu (7 sites)

RECOMMENDED TRIP OPTION: Leave your vehicle at Whakapapa Village and walk to Mangatepopo Hut, staying there and then at Oturere and Waihohonu. While you are advised to start early from Mangatepopo to beat the crowds walking the Tongariro Alpine Crossing (most of which shares a day-long section of the Great Walk), this option does allow you to take your time on the rest of the track and to do lots of exploring along the way.

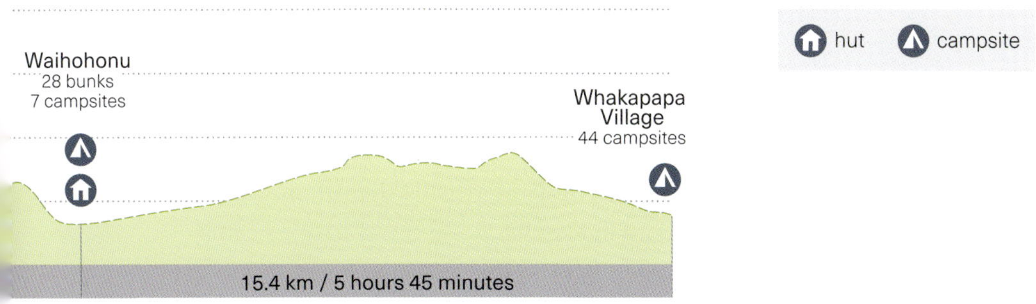

The track up past Mangatepopo Hut.

PLANNING

ACCESS: The Tongariro Northern Circuit can be easily reached by road and rail. Trains and buses both stop at the nearby village of National Park, and if you don't have a vehicle there is a shuttle operating from the Whakapapa Holiday Park to get you to Whakapapa Village.

The track is accessible from four points, with Whakapapa Village being the main entrance and exit point. There is plenty of parking in the village, and from there it is approximately a 3 hour walk to Mangatepopo Hut, or a 5–6 hour walk to Waihohonu Hut.

There is also access to the track and a parking area at the end of Mangatepopo Road, but note that this gets particularly busy with people doing the Tongariro Alpine Crossing, and there is currently a four-hour parking limit. From the car park it is approximately a 30 minute walk to Mangatepopo Hut.

Ketetahi Road on the northern side of Mt Tongariro is the other end of the Tongariro Alpine Crossing and will also likely be busy. From here it is a 2–3 hour walk to Ketetahi Shelter (not available for accommodation

Mangatepopo Hut.

since the 2012 eruption), and then a further 3 hours to Oturere Hut on the Tongariro Northern Circuit or 4–5 hours over the crossing back to Mangatepopo Hut.

A less-used access is off the Desert Road (SH1), about 35 kilometres south of Tūrangi and on the eastern side of Tongariro. From the car park it takes around 1 hour 30 minutes to walk to Waihohonu Hut.

ACCOMMODATION, FOOD AND EQUIPMENT: The nearest accommodation is at Whakapapa Village, and there is more at nearby National Park and Tūrangi. There is a choice of places to eat at Whakapapa Village, and a few food supplies can be purchased at the Whakapapa Holiday Park if you prefer to cook. A larger shop is at National Park, 10 kilometres away.

WEATHER: This is an elevated part of the North Island (the track starts at around 1000 m) and so is open to very changeable conditions. Parts of the track are particularly exposed to what will sometimes be extreme mountain weather (strong winds, rain and snow). Check the forecast beforehand and ask at the DOC visitor centre or one of the DOC officers stationed at the huts if you are unsure about conditions ahead.

Devil's Staircase leading up to the South Crater.

TRACK CONDITIONS: Much of this track crosses an alpine environment and should be treated with the appropriate level of respect and caution. It is exposed to high winds, low visibility and the possibility of snow at any time of year. In poor conditions it may be advisable to turn around rather than risk carrying on – ask a DOC officer if you are unsure.

OTHER HAZARDS: Please note that you will be entering active volcano country. The mountains and the varied landscapes beneath them exist because of previous eruptions, and the changing environment affects walking conditions. For instance, debris from the last eruption (in 2012) hit Ketetahi Hut (now a day shelter). Take the time to visit the DOC visitor centre and speak to the staff at Whakapapa Village to familiarise yourself with what might happen in the event of an eruption and the safety precautions you might need to take.

Note, too, that during this trip you will likely come across scores of inappropriately dressed day walkers attempting the Tongariro Crossing. Plainly put, these people are a disaster waiting to happen! While on a warm, still summer's day, conditions on the crossing can be rather pleasant, remember this is an alpine environment where the weather can deteriorate drastically and rapidly. Make sure you read the clothing section at the beginning of this guide and pack appropriately.

TRACK DESCRIPTION

Starting from Whakapapa Village, the Tongariro Northern Circuit can be walked in either direction. But, given that the 3 hour stretch from Whakapapa Village to Mangatepopo Hut has not been well maintained and tends to be heavily eroded and rough underfoot, it is possible to leave your vehicle at the village and take a short shuttle to the road end below Mangatepopo Hut and start there.

Mangatepopo Hut to Emerald Lakes: 3–4 hrs, 8 km

This part of the track shares the Tongariro Alpine Crossing and so can be very busy with day walkers. Once past Mangatepopo Hut (only 30 minutes

The South Crater can often be covered with snow.

from the car park), a very well-formed track follows Mangatepopo Stream up the valley, heading towards Ngāuruhoe and eventually ascending into an alpine environment over a series of old lava flows. The youngest lava flows – the blackest – erupted from Ngāuruhoe in 1949 and again in 1954.

From the head of the valley, there is a steeper but still well-graded climb known as the Devil's Staircase, which leads up to Mangatepopo Saddle and the surprisingly flat terrain of South Crater. Look behind you for views back down the valley and, on a clear day, of another volcano, Mt Taranaki, in the distance to the west. From the saddle the track crosses South Crater (not a true crater, but rather a drainage basin tucked between the bulk of Tongariro and Ngāuruhoe).

The trail from South Crater carries on up a ridge towards Red Crater; it is steep and can be slippery underfoot. Care must be taken here, especially in windy or freezing conditions, as the slopes either side of the track may be slippery or icy even if the track itself is ice-free. Follow the marker poles up the ridge to a junction where the main track continues past the rim of Red Crater, in good visibility offering views of Oturere Valley below you and the Kaimanawa Ranges out to the east. This is the high point of the track. From here, your path descends a steep debris slope to the Emerald Lakes. Again, be careful here if the wind is strong or the terrain icy.

The view of Emerald Lakes is worth the effort.

Emerald Lakes to Oturere Hut: 1.5 hrs, 5 km

While the Tongariro Alpine Crossing continues across the Central Crater, the Tongariro Northern Circuit branches off at the aptly named Emerald Lakes before descending steeply into the Oturere Valley. The number of people on the track should lessen considerably, allowing you more space to enjoy your surroundings. Some of this terrain can also be slippery or unstable underfoot. You may want to pause to take in the many different lava formations created from past eruptions in the Red Crater area, and which contributed to filling the Oturere Valley. This is a quite mystical place to travel through, and is especially eerie on a misty day with the strange, gargoyle-like formations rising around you.

Oturere Hut is set on the eastern edge of these old lava flows, and the setting offers great views across the Rangipō Desert. There is also a waterfall just over the ridge from the hut.

Oturere Hut to Waihohonu Hut: 3 hrs, 9 km

With the ever-present cone of Ngāuruhoe above you, the track traverses a series of shallow valleys and ridges – undulating terrain, but never too

There are pockets of forest between Oturere Hut and Waihohonu Hut and again near the end of the track.

taxing – before making a sharp descent into a branch of Waihohonu Stream and some of the only beech forest (or any forest) you will come across other than that close to Whakapapa Village. You may hear the thin peeps of riflemen – or, if you're really lucky, see the tiny birds as they flitter between branches over you. You climb back up through the forest to an open ridge line, before descending into another small section of forest and, finally, the rather plush Waihohonu Hut.

Waihohonu Hut to Whakapapa Village: 5–6 hrs, 15 km

The broad country between Ngāuruhoe and Ruapehu is open and exposed. At first, the track follows the Waihohonu Stream, past a short (10 minute) detour to the old Waihohonu Hut, and then it gradually climbs to the broad Tama Saddle. This area can get particularly windy, owing to the funnelling effect of the mountains.

From the saddle, and now only 2 hours from finishing at Whakapapa Village, there is a very pleasant side trip to the Tama Lakes. These are two infilled explosion craters; the lower lake (at around 1200 m) is only 10 minutes from the junction, but to reach the upper lake you will need

Lower Tama Lake.

to climb a further 40 minutes up a steep ridge. The lakes are named after Tamatea, the high chief of the Tākitimu waka, who was believed to have travelled through this landscape around 600 years ago.

From the Tama Lakes turn-off, the last portion of the track is particularly well formed. You may catch sight of the village from the top of a steady rise, but there is still a way to go, along with a choice of finishes. The more interesting track passes underneath Taranaki Falls, before a nice section of forest and the final easy stretch to the village.

POINTS OF INTEREST

A park of ages

Tongariro National Park is this country's oldest national park. The summits of the peaks were provided in a tuku, or transaction, by the great chief Horonuku Te Heuheu Tukino IV to the people of New Zealand in 1887. Te Heuheu Tukino was a pragmatic man. Not wanting the land of Ngāti Tūwharetoa to be divided up and sold for farming and logging, he gifted the peaks to the Crown to preserve their spiritual significance. The original gift was 2360 hectares, and in the following years the government purchased or otherwise obtained surrounding land, increasing the park size to its current 79,598 hectares. In 1990 the park was given World Heritage status, in recognition of its natural and cultural values, and in 1993 it gained additional standing – in effect, acquiring dual World Heritage status – on account of its intangible cultural associations.

Along with the growth of the park came the growth of tourism. The first commercial guiding may have been provided by the Allan brothers as early as 1895. These days tourism is big business to the local communities dotted around the base of the mountains. International visitors arrive by the busload, hoping the weather stays clear long enough for them to see the mountains, perhaps complete a hike over the flank of Tongariro, and in winter grab a snow day at either Whakapapa or Tūroa ski fields. The Department of Conservation does a sterling job of maintaining the extensive track and hut system zigzagging through much of the park, and also of the volcano monitoring system, which offers a level of security for anyone in the park.

The height of a mountain

Mt Ruapehu, the highest point in the North Island, used to be higher still before major eruptions demolished the top portion of its volcanic cone. Eruptions have occurred here, and are likely to continue to occur, every five to 10 years, with larger ones every 20 to 50 years. Ruapehu is the most active of the three major volcanoes in the area, and considered the most active volcano on mainland New Zealand. Over the years, it has had some spectacular – and dangerous – eruptions and lahar flows. Since 1945, more than 17 eruptions and 60 lahars have been recorded.

An active land

Mt Ruapehu's Crater Lake contains up to 10 million cubic metres of acidic water. Crater Lake is one of only a handful known in the world where the andesitic magma and glacial melt-water combine, and sometimes produce spectacular eruptions. In 1953 the Crater Lake burst, sending a lahar down the flanks of the volcano. The torrent swept away the Tangiwai railway bridge, minutes before a crowded train was due to cross. One hundred and fifty-three people lost their lives in the resulting tragedy, which remains New Zealand's worst rail disaster. After the Tangiwai incident, the first of this country's lahar warning systems was installed. Over the years, and after more eruptions, the warning systems have been repeatedly upgraded.

In 1995 and 1996 Mt Ruapehu erupted on a number of occasions, sending volcanic rock and ash clouds high into the air. Then in 2007, young climbers William Pike and James Christie were staying in Dome Shelter, not far from Crater Lake, when a small eruption occurred. William was pinned when flying rubble hit the shelter, and James had to rush down the mountain in the dark for help. William lost his leg in the accident.

And then in 2012 Mt Tongariro erupted, sending rocks crashing into the nearby Ketetahi Hut and forcing DOC to close the Tongariro Alpine Crossing. Luckily no one was staying in the hut at the time. Adventuring here brings with it a whole new set of risks outside of the normal weather, avalanche and rockfall considerations of being in the mountains.

Fauna and flora

Given such a contrasting landscape, it's no surprise that this is home to a wide range of flora. The impact of past volcanic events can be seen in the charred tree stumps scattered along parts of the Rangipō Desert, and much of this harsh land of old lava flows and other volcanic debris has only alpine grasses, flax and stunted hebe as its main established plant life. For the avid plant enthusiast this may be an oddly intriguing environment, but most people are likely to prefer the more obvious beech forests and wide tussock fields to the west of the three mountains.

Native birds are plentiful in the park. In forested areas you may see the bellbird, tūī, robin, tomtit and fantail, as well as New Zealand's smallest bird, the rifleman. You might be lucky enough to spot the whio (blue duck) in a stream. In open terrain you may see the pipit, the rarer kārearea (New Zealand falcon), and maybe a kākā, and even some wayward seagulls that reside in the area in summer.

Taranaki Falls.

OFF THE TRACK

If the Tongariro Northern Circuit isn't enough for you, or if you are waiting out a period of bad weather, a range of other trips can be done from Whakapapa Village. The DOC visitor centre has information on all of the local tracks, as well a range of displays that will keep you entertained on a wet morning or afternoon.

Visit Taranaki Falls

A 2 hour circuit starts and finishes at Whakapapa Village, leading through forest up to the base of the falls and then traversing back across slopes above it.

Walk the Whakapapanui Track

This 2 hour return walk starts around 250 metres from the visitor centre, traversing through beech forest and along the banks of the Whakapapanui River.

Trek to Tama Lakes

These pristine lakes can easily be done in a day from Whakapapa Village. Allow 5 hours for the round trip.

Tackle the Tongariro Alpine Crossing

If you are keen enough to join the crowds, this is an awesome experience – one of the best day trips in New Zealand's mountains! Leave your car at Whakapapa Village and use one of the local shuttle services to get you to and from each end of the track (recent parking restrictions make this a necessity).

Hike the Ruapehu Round the Mountain Track

This is a much longer, much more demanding and much less used track than any of the previous options. Taking 4–6 days, it traverses a range of landscapes, and while they are similar to those on the Northern Circuit, with areas of dense beech forest and wide alpine tussock fields, there are

Mt Ruapehu is a constant presence on the southern section of the track.

places where you might feel further away from civilisation, if that's what you're after. Overall, the length of track allows the walker more time to enjoy the back-country experience. While the track is well signposted and poled, be aware that in places it is unformed and can be difficult to follow in poor visibility or snow. Given that it crosses through alpine terrain, this track should be attempted only between December and April unless you have specific mountaineering experience. Check conditions with DOC beforehand.

Enjoy the meandering water of the Whanganui.

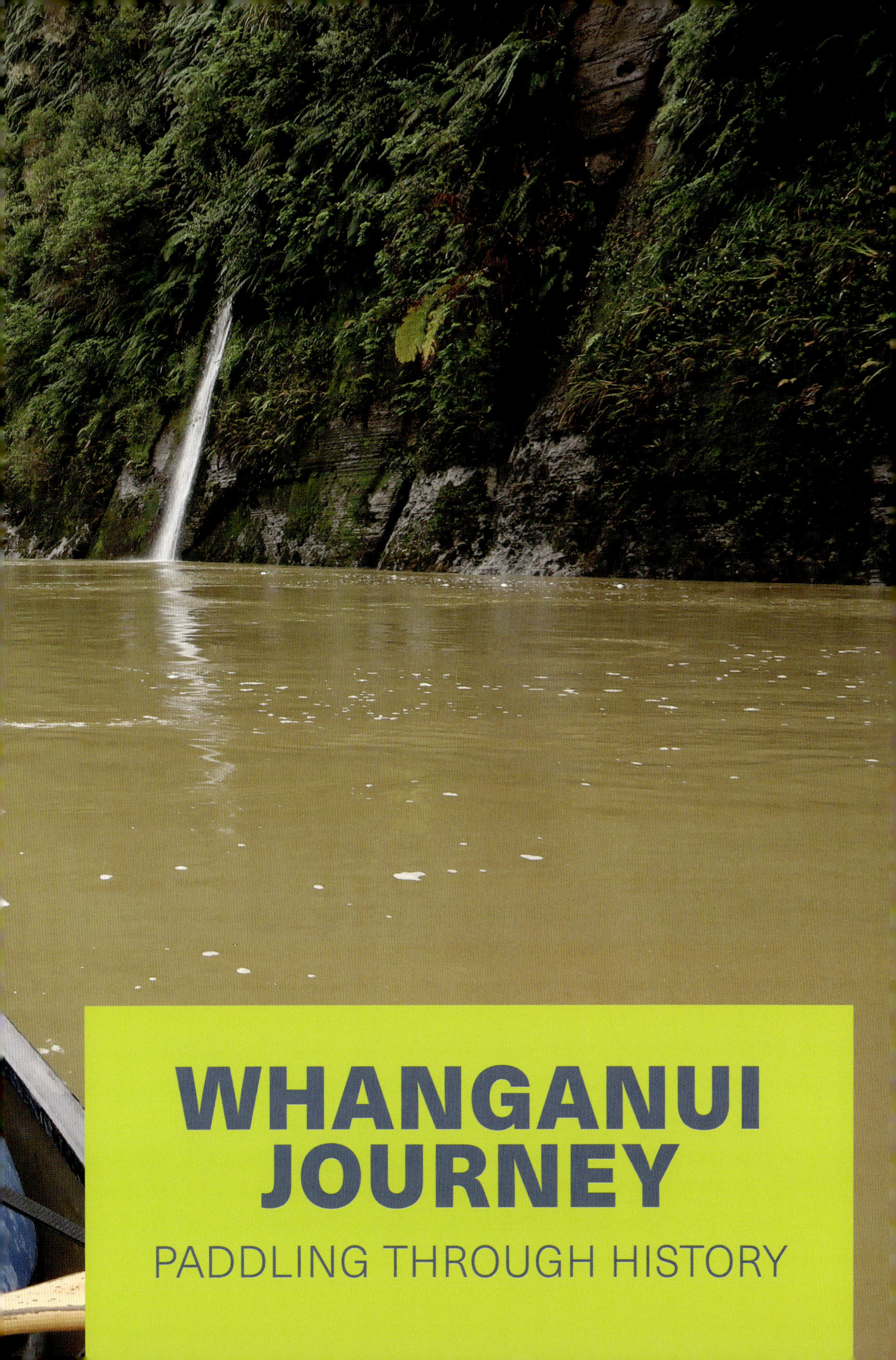

WHANGANUI JOURNEY

PADDLING THROUGH HISTORY

WHANGANUI JOURNEY

PADDLING THROUGH HISTORY // 145 KM, 3–5 DAYS

KO AU TE AWA, KO TE AWA KO AU.
I AM THE RIVER AND THE RIVER IS ME.

— MĀORI WHAKATAUĀKĪ / PROVERB

— HIGHLIGHTS

- Spend up to five unique days on New Zealand's longest navigable river (or ten if you choose to paddle all the way to Whanganui).
- Take a side trip to the famous Bridge to Nowhere.
- Relax in remote, picturesque campsites far from any roads or settlements.
- Experience the protocols and traditions of a riverside marae.
- Explore the local Māori and Pākehā history.

THE GREAT SERPENT of water that is the Whanganui River emerges from the western slopes of Mt Tongariro. The river percolates through the land, twisting between rock outcrops, then arching and slicing through farmland and forest across the middle of the North Island. At first it flows north-west towards the town of Taumarunui, before turning to the south, south-east and finally south-west, dispersing into the Tasman Sea 290 kilometres from its source.

This water carries with it tales and travellers. For centuries local Māori have paddled the river by canoe, built their homes on its banks, fished on it and fought over it. These days, to be privileged enough to travel downstream is to immerse yourself in the history of the surrounding land as well as the people who once lived here and who still live here.

The third-longest river in New Zealand (behind the Waikato and the Clutha), the Whanganui has been granted special status due to its significance to the region's Māori. In 2017 it was given its own legal identity

N
Taumarunui
Cherry Grove
to Turang
41
43
Ōhinepane
Te Maire Bridge
Whanganui Riv
4
Ōnura River
Poukaria
Kirikau Landing
Ōwhango
Stratford
Maharanui
4
Retaruke River
Kirikiriroa Peninsula
Whakahoro
Raurimu
Mangapapa
Tangarakau River
Heao Strm
Whanganui River
Ōhauora
National Park
47
John Coull
Mangapurua Valley
4
hangamomona R.
Bridge to Nowhere
Mangawaiiti
Mangapūrua
Tieke Kāinga
MATEMATEĀONGA RANGE
Manganuioteao River
49
Raetihi
Ōhakune
Ngāporo
Pipiriki
4
to Whanganui
0
5
10 km

(the second natural landscape with this status after Te Urewera), which means it has the same rights as a person. This groundbreaking Treaty settlement brought a long-running litigation between the Crown and tangata whenua to an end.

The Whanganui Journey covers 145 kilometres of the river, much of it passing through the Whanganui National Park. This Great Walk has an obvious difference to other tracks covered in the book. Rather than trekking overland, you are paddling and drifting down a river in a canoe or kayak, easing between steep-walled canyons, exploring side streams, resting at beaches, and always travelling at a pace the river dictates.

There are numerous small rapids to negotiate, and then long stretches of calm water where it feels as though you are hardly moving at all. The realisation that, for much of the journey, there are no roads nearby will enhance your sense of being distanced from the outside world. Instead, paddling and camping, listening to birdsong and taking in the scenery becomes your everyday life – for a few memorable days, at least.

At one section of the river you are able to leave your canoe and take a short walk to the aptly named Bridge to Nowhere. Spanning a gorge, this concrete road bridge seems completely isolated from any signs of civilisation. It was constructed back in 1936 to help with access to a settlement in the Mangapūrua Valley. But the area was abandoned in 1942, which meant the bridge was only in use for six years. Today it forms part of the Te Araroa walking trail and the Mountains to Sea cycle trail, as well as providing a welcome side trip for river voyagers.

In low flow especially, there are lots of beaches to stop at.

The history of the Whanganui River is a huge part of what makes this Great 'Walk' special. It is indeed a privilege to be able to experience a journey such as this, and to appreciate everything that has happened here in the past. Embrace the knowledge that, for a time, you have become a part of the river and the river has become a part of you.

TRACK DETAILS

LOCATION: Whanganui National Park (Central North Island)
TRACK TYPE: The river is generally only paddled in one direction: downstream. The 145 kilometre journey from Taumarunui to Pipiriki takes on average 5 days to complete by canoe. A shorter 3 day journey from Whakahoro to Pipiriki is also possible. For the 5 day trip most people plan to spend the night at Ōhinepane, Whakahoro, John Coull and Tieke Kāinga campsites, but note that there are a number of other campsites spread along the river if these are busy.

START POINT: Taumarunui for the 5 day trip and Whakahoro for the 3 day trip.
END POINT: Pipiriki
DISTANCE: 145 km
TIME: 3–5 days
SEASON: It is recommended that the river be paddled during the open season, currently 1 October – 30 April. Outside of this time it is more likely to be flooded and there are fewer options for help if you get into trouble. Only very experienced kayakers and canoeists should consider attempting it during the off season.
GRADING: Moderate fitness and paddling skills required
DOC HUTS: John Coull (24 bunks). Note there is also the option of staying at Tieke Kāinga Marae (20 bunks)
DOC CAMPSITES: Ōhinepane (36 sites), Poukaria (12 sites), Maharanui (12 sites), Whakahoro (36 sites), Mangapapa (17 sites), Ōhauora (20 sites), John Coull (26 sites), Mangawaiiti (26 sites), Mangapūrua (10 sites), Tieke Kāinga (28 sites), Ngāporo (32 sites)

RECOMMENDED TRIP OPTION: Leave your vehicle (or public transport) somewhere central like Ōhakune, hire a canoe and any other necessary gear, and get the hire company to drop you off and pick you up (Canoe Safaris in Ōhakune is a good option, but there are other choices). Take the 5 day trip, camping at Ōhinepane and Whakahoro, then staying at John Coull Hut and Tieke Kāinga Marae. Note that with the 5 day option there are no huts for the first 2 nights, so you will have to camp.

John Coull Hut.

PLANNING

ACCESS: Access points for the start of the journey are at Ngahuinga in Taumarunui (Cherry Grove), Ōhinepane (access from River Road, SH43), and Whakahoro (access from Raurimu or Ōwhango). The main exit point is at Pipiriki (with access from Raetihi). The beginning and end of the journey are a long way apart, so you are advised to leave your vehicle somewhere secure and arrange to be dropped off and picked up by one of the local support companies.

ACCOMMODATION, FOOD AND EQUIPMENT: Equipment hire (canoe and watertight containers) and other services (including guides if needed) along with food and transport can be found in Taumarunui, Whanganui, Raetihi, Ōhakune and National Park village. There are airports at Whanganui and Taupō, and a range of public road transport options throughout the region.

WEATHER: It is important to understand the implications of changes in weather, especially if you are paddling the Whanganui without a guide.

Numerous side streams and rivers allow opportunity to explore.

Rainfall in any of the main tributaries, which might be a long way from the Whanganui, can still affect the river level greatly. Check with one of the local hiring or guiding companies if you are not sure.

RIVER CONDITIONS: In low flow this is a pleasant river to paddle down, with over 200 mostly small and easily managed rapids to provide entertainment and excitement without being dangerous. Also, there are plenty of beaches to stop at and sort yourself if you have tipped out. When the river is in higher flow it runs much faster and most of the beaches disappear. Again, if you are not confident of your ability, consider using a guide for your journey.

OTHER CONSIDERATIONS: Paddling a river requires different safety equipment to tramping on land. No doubt your hire company (if you use one) will inform and kit you out properly, but be sure to take life jackets, waterproof containers, a laminated map/river guide, wetsuits (depending on time of year), a bailer and a spare paddle. Note that there is very little cellphone coverage on the river. Once you have committed to it, your only reliable form of communication in an emergency is a PLB device.

Tamatea's Cave.

However, it is likely that you will not be the only users on the Whanganui. Jet boats travel up and down the river. If you hear them coming it is advisable to move to the side of the river (to the true right if possible) and, if needed, point the nose of your canoe or kayak directly across their wake to lessen its effect on your craft.

JOURNEY DESCRIPTION

Taumarunui to Ōhinepane: 3–5 hrs, 22 km

This is a relatively short day and an opportunity to get your paddling technique and communication sorted. The launch point at Cherry Grove is at the confluence of the Whanganui and Ōngarue rivers – look for the boat ramp. As you travel the upper section of the river you will pass mostly through areas of farmland (which are not part of the Whanganui National Park) as well as pockets of native bush. There are some early rapids to boost your excitement levels, and keep an eye out for Te Maire bridge (the only bridge across the Whanganui between here and Pipiriki), which is around half an hour before the Ōhinepane Campsite.

Ōhinepane to Whakahoro: 6–8 hrs, 35 km

Prepare for a fuller day's paddling, and also a feeling of entering a more remote landscape. There are fewer roads nearby, and the farmland gives way to larger areas of forest. Keep watch for Kirikau Landing, which at one time was the highest inland stop for the steamer service from the coastal settlement of Whanganui.

If you feel like stopping earlier, campsites along the river are on offer at Poukaria and Maharanui, before finally reaching Whakahoro. Note that if the water is running a little high, there could be a standing wave at the confluence with the Ōhura tributary, which has a large catchment.

Whakahoro to John Coull Hut: 7–9 hrs, 37.5 km

Depending on where you've chosen to spend the night, this could be your longest day paddling on the river. Some people decide to start their trip at Whakahoro, entering the Retaruke tributary and getting used to their canoe before committing to the much larger Whanganui. From now on you are committed to the journey, as there is no more road access between here and Pipiriki at the end.

On either side of the river is the thick forest of Whanganui National Park. Bird calls might echo down, and occasionally kererū can be seen winging across the watery gap. Mangapapa Campsite, at the start of the long and narrow Kirikiriroa Peninsula, is a nice place to stop for a rest, or you could push on to the next campsite, Ōhauora. In low flow, this section of river is a mixture of short easy rapids and long sections of slow-moving water, and it can be a struggle making progress against any headwind. After rains, the nature of the river is more that of a fast-flowing boil of water, transferring you much more quickly down to your overnight stop at the John Coull hut and campsite.

Mangawaiiti Campsite.

John Coull Hut to Tieke Kāinga: 4–6 hrs, 29 km

The Whanganui National Park spreads over an area of around 750 square kilometres. The denseness of the forest, lining either side of the river below John Coull Hut, makes you feel like you are a long way from anywhere. The Tangarakau on the right-hand side is the first major tributary you will pass on this day, and you may be able to paddle a short distance up it as a side trip. Further down is the Whangamomona River, which you can also explore without leaving your canoe. Not far beyond the Whangamomona, the Mangawaiiti Campsite is set high above the banks of the river on the right-hand side. A small, grassy platform held in a cusp of forest, it is a great place to pull up your canoe and climb the clay steps for lunch.

Further downriver, the Bridge to Nowhere walk is a must-do side trip, a mere half-hour walk (one way) from the landing. Be aware that jet boats travel upriver to this point for the walk, and the track is also part of the Mountains to Sea Cycle Trail and the Te Araroa Trail.

Tieke Kāinga Marae is a great place to spend the night; whether you're in the campground or on the marae, you can be sure of enjoying the local hospitality.

The landing site for a side trip to the Bridge to Nowhere.

WHANGA
PIPIRIKI NEW ZEALAND
PIPIRIKI NEW ZEALAND
Welcome Aboard..

Tieke Kāinga to Pipiriki: 3–5 hrs, 21.5 km

This is the last day of your journey, but also potentially the most exciting, with a number of rapids to negotiate before reaching the end at Pipiriki. The Manganui ō te Ao River is worth a side trip, paddling against the current up to the first rapid; you may be lucky enough to see the whio (rare blue duck).

The section below the Ngāporo Campsite is the most concentrated area of rapids. None of them are major, but they do have the potential to tip you out if you're not paying enough attention to your entry points into them. The vegetation changes markedly just before you reach Pipiriki, with farmland and pine trees visible on the hills above, before one final rapid to test you just above the boat ramp exit on the left of the river.

POINTS OF INTEREST

The stories of a place

Māori legend explains the forming of the Whanganui River, along with the location of the volcanic mountains spread over the North Island. Once, many volcanoes gathered in the centre of the North Island. Taranaki, Tongariro, Ngāuruhoe, Ruapehu, Pūtauaki and Tauhara competed for the attention of the bush-clad Mt Pihanga. Tongariro, the dominant mountain, fought with the next strongest, Taranaki, over Pihanga. Fires burned from their summits and smoke clouded the sky. Tongariro lost his head in the battle, which fell into Lake Taupō and can still be seen as Motutaiko Island, while Taranaki received a blow that took a huge chunk from his side.

Eventually, Tongariro defeated Taranaki, banishing him and the other mountains. Pūtauaki travelled north to the edge of the Kaingaroa Plain, while Tauhara moved east as far as Lake Taupō. But Taranaki, whose love for Pihanga was said to be the strongest, ventured the furthest, gouging a channel as he followed the setting sun as far as he could. When Taranaki left the central plateau for the coast, the land was split open, and the Whanganui River formed, filling the rift that Taranaki had created.

According to locals, the Whanganui was first explored by Tamatea, one of the leaders of the original migration to the new land, and he was said to

The Bridge to Nowhere is an easy 30-minute walk from the river.

have travelled up the river and on to Lake Taupō. There are a number of sites along the river that are named in honour of Tamatea and his journey.

A river and its people

Just as the Whanganui River cuts its winding path for hundreds of kilometres across the North Island, so, too, winds its long history of associated human travel and settlement. And, not surprisingly, the river still holds huge significance for Māori.

Small pā (settlements) from the iwi Te Ātihaunui were spread up and down the river from around AD 1100, with travel between them by waka (canoe) relatively easy. Amid a backdrop of dense forest, inhabitants of the pā hunted birds, developed terraces above the river for planting vegetables, and caught freshwater eels with their hīnaki (wicker traps).

But the living here wouldn't have been easy. Battles between settlements were common, especially when competition for land and resources intensified. As each settlement grew, and still before the arrival of Pākehā in Aotearoa, the Whanganui was believed to have been one of the most densely populated areas in the Central North Island.

Slowly and inevitably after their arrival, Pākehā spread inland from their first land purchase and settlement on the coast (at the town of Whanganui). They established their own trade up the river, which, in the absence of good roads, offered the easiest route to the interior of the island. A regular steamboat service began in 1892, and at one stage operated as far inland as Taumarunui. From there, various coaches travelled to other parts of the interior. Within a few years, travel up the Whanganui had become a major tourist attraction in itself; but as the railway network developed early in the new century, demand for the steamboat journey declined.

Over the years, various farming operations were attempted, using the river and then remote roads for access. The most famous is probably the aforementioned Bridge to Nowhere settlement of Mangapūrua, which was established for soldiers returning from World War I, but later abandoned, owing to the difficulty of access and the rugged terrain.

The land and nature

As can be seen from the deep gorges cut by the river's path, the sandstones and mudstones forming this landscape have been greatly eroded over time. The local forests are predominantly broadleaf–podocarp, with rātā, kāmahi, rimu and tawa among the more established giants. There are also areas of beech trees, and a range of North Island birds populating them. At each campsite it is worth going for a walk through the surrounding forest to listen to their calls and see what species you can spot. And, each night, listen out for brown kiwi: you may hear a piping whistle from the male, and a hoarse croak from the female.

OFF THE TRACK

Lake Surprise Track: 5 hrs, 12 km

If you are based in Ōhakune and have a day to spare, this track, which is part of the Ruapehu Round the Mountain track, is well worth a walk. Starting 15 kilometres up the Ohakune Mountain Road, just below the car park for Tūroa Ski Field, the track sidles down and then across an open

Countless waterfalls
tumble into the river.

Tieke Kāinga Marae.

volcanic landscape, following a well-marked track, before descending into Mangatururturu Valley via a scramble over photogenic silica bedrock that flows beneath a river. After getting to Mangatururturu Hut, you cross the unbridged Mangatururturu River (which can also rise quickly in flood) before climbing again above the valley. Arriving at Lake Surprise – a shallow lake set among beech forest and tussock – is literally a surprise.

Te Araroa Trail: 4 days, 89 km

A section of this trail, which traverses the length of New Zealand, passes through a portion of the Whanganui National Park. Start at National Park (note that some of the trail is on unsealed roads, before reaching Whakahoro). From Whakahoro to Mangapūrua Landing is around 40 kilometres of track running mostly through the national park, and also crossing the Bridge to Nowhere. At Mangapūrua Landing you will require a boat trip down part of the river to Pipiriki. Check the website, www.teararoa.org.nz, for more detailed information.

Mountains to Sea Cycle Trail: 3 days, 200 km

From the fringes of Mt Ruapehu to the coastal shores of Whanganui, this route encompasses two national parks as well as the Whanganui River. (The total distance cited above includes 30 kilometres by jet boat.) Starting at the Ohakune Mountain Road, the trail takes in the alpine grandeur of the central plateau, and runs along historic bridle trails. Like the Te Araroa section, this trail also crosses the Bridge to Nowhere and requires transport down the Whanganui River to land at Pipiriki. From there, carry on down the Whanganui River Road, eventually reaching the city of Whanganui on the coast. Check the website, www.mountainstosea.co.nz, for more detailed information.

Stunning beaches along the Abel Tasman offer plenty of opportunities to relax.

ABEL TASMAN COAST TRACK

THE GOLDEN HIGHWAY

ABEL TASMAN COAST TRACK

THE GOLDEN HIGHWAY // 60 KM, 3–5 DAYS

HIGHLIGHTS

- Camp at any one of a number of beautiful beachside tent sites.
- Enjoy the unique mix of bush and beach tramping.
- Take in a varied perspective of the park, travelling by kayak or boat or on foot.
- Swim in the ocean at the end of each day's travel.
- Appreciate the endless beaches, all encouraging you not to rush.

LIKE SLIVERS OF sunlight nestled into a cusp of clearest blue ocean and then backed by the deep greens of native forest, the beaches of Abel Tasman National Park are without doubt jewels in the crown of the South Island. Set between rocky headlands that jut along the coastline between Tasman Bay and Golden Bay, these golden-sand beaches make up much of the Abel Tasman Coast Track.

This Great Walk and the national park itself may be explored in many different ways – more than simply tramping – and all variations produce the opportunity for an enjoyable mix of physical exertion and hedonistic beach life. In summer especially it is advisable to punctuate the journey of walking or kayaking through the park with prolonged bouts of swimming, snorkelling and sunbathing.

Inland, rivers and streams run through woodlands and valleys; eventually they join the sea, where rock formations abut headlands topped mostly in established or regenerating native forest. Bird calls carry through the trees, and seals can be seen sunbathing on rocky outcrops and feeding and playing in the ocean.

People have been visiting or living here for hundreds of years. At a half-moon of golden sand that is Te Pukatea Bay, a track leads up Pitt Head to

0
5
10 km
Separation Point
Whariwharangi
Mutton Cove
Golden Bay
Wainui Bay
Wainui Bay
Anapai Bay
Tōtaranui
Pohara
Waiharakeke Bay
Awaroa Head
Tākaka
Awaroa Inlet
Awaroa
Tonga Saddle
Onetahuti Bay
Tonga Island
Tonga Quarry
PIKIKIRUNA RANGE
Mosquito Bay
Bark Bay
Bark Bay
Cascade Falls
Falls River
Torrent Bay Village
Torrent Bay
Pitt Head
Te Pukatea Bay
Cleopatra's Pool
Anchorage
Observation Beach
Watering Cove
Akersten Bay
Apple Tree Bay
Adele Island
Coquille Bay
Tinline
Fisherman Island
Sandy Bay
Marahau
60
N
Tākaka
to Motueka

an ancient Māori pā site. The terracing from the pā and old food pits can still be seen. At the top, taking in a view that stretches in all directions, you'll easily see why the headland was chosen as a defensive location.

The track is easily walkable at any time of the year, and the water's generally warm enough for a dip between December and March. Expect to see lots of other walkers and day visitors, especially in summer, although the northern stretch of the track (between Tōtaranui and Wainui Bay) is less frequented, as the water taxi service is almost non-existent in this area and guided groups are limited. Four comfortable huts service the track, but for a more fulfilling experience it is recommended you take a tent and camp under the stars – there are a total of 19 campsites thoughtfully spaced along the coast to choose from.

As a Great Walk experience, the Abel Tasman Coast Track is both intriguing and relaxing. The only track that predominately follows a coastline, it allows walkers and kayakers a unique perspective on a beautiful corner of New Zealand, an area that has been protected for all to experience and enjoy. (Much of the sea life nearby is protected under the Tonga Island Marine Reserve, created in 1993.) And, while parts of the track may seem tame when compared to some of the other Great Walks, this only adds to the feeling of wanting to relax and take your time.

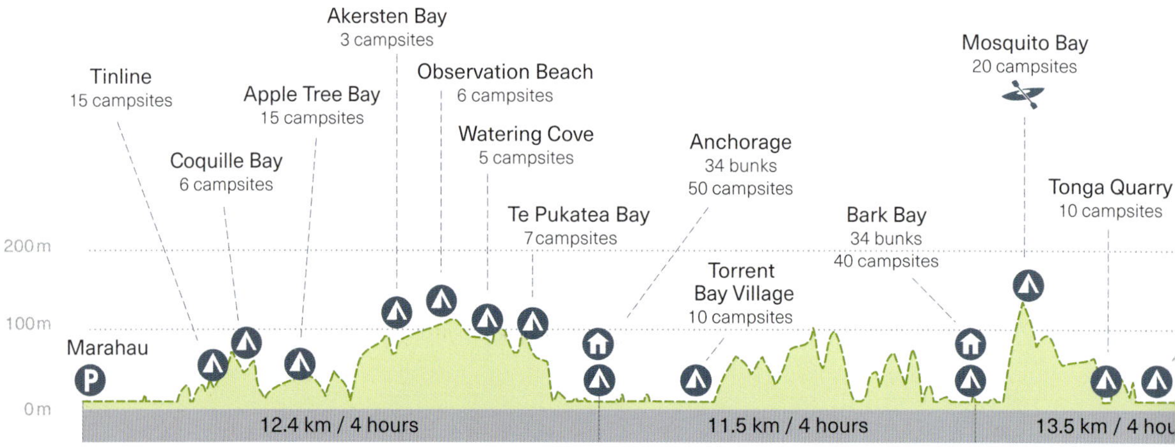

Local operators offer drop-offs and pick-ups at a number of beaches.

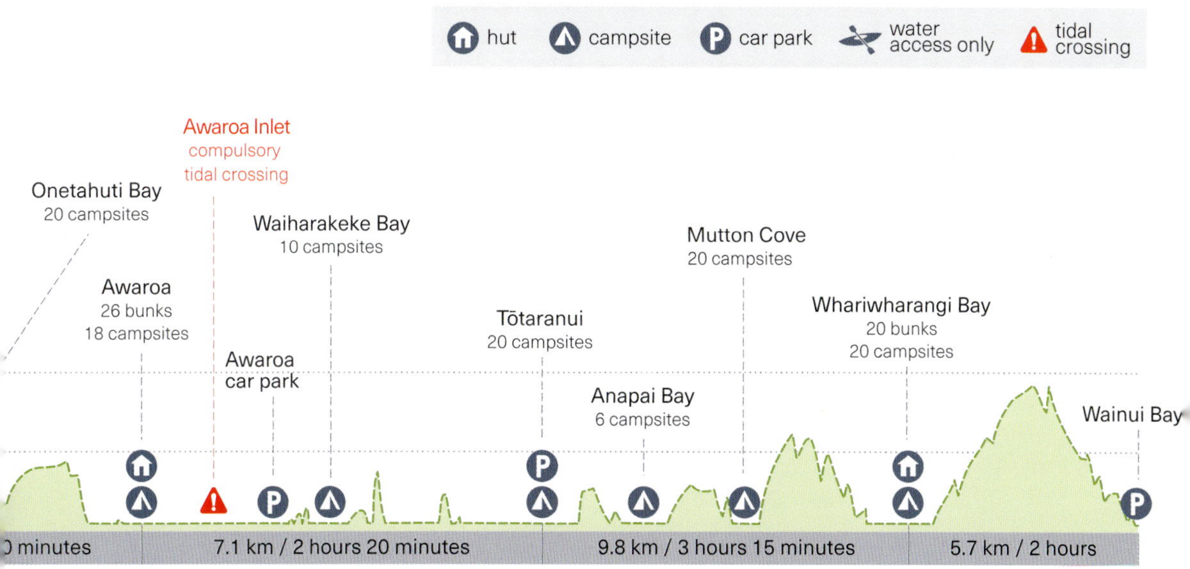

TRACK DETAILS

LOCATION: Abel Tasman National Park, Nelson
TRACK TYPE: This is a through track and can be walked (or kayaked) in either direction. Travel on the track is undulating rather than taxing, with no major hill climbs and plenty of beautiful beaches to relax at.

START POINT: Marahau or Wainui Bay
END POINT: Wainui Bay or Marahau
DISTANCE: 60 km
TIME: 3–5 days
SEASON: All year round (there is a peak season in terms of hut and campsite costs)
GRADING: Easy to moderate fitness required
DOC HUTS: There are four huts: Anchorage (34 bunks), Bark Bay (34 bunks), Awaroa (26 bunks) and Whariwharangi Bay (20 bunks)
DOC CAMPSITES: Tinline (15 sites), Coquille Bay (6 sites), Apple Tree Bay (15 sites), Akersten Bay (3 sites), Observation Beach (6 sites), Watering Cove (5 sites), Te Pukatea Bay (7 sites), Anchorage (50 sites), Torrent Bay Village (10 sites), Bark Bay (40 sites), Mosquito Bay (20 sites), Tonga Quarry (10 sites), Onetahuti Bay (20 sites), Awaroa (18 sites), Waiharakeke (10 sites), Tōtaranui (20 sites), Anapai Bay (6 sites), Mutton Cove (20 sites), Whariwharangi (20 sites)

RECOMMENDED TRIP OPTION: For the slightly more adventurous, the dream trip is to kayak in one direction and walk back the other. This will require some organising with the kayak and transport providers but is certainly doable if you have the time and inclination. Otherwise, walk in one direction and get a boat back. Whichever way you do the track and however long you take, the quintessential Abel Tasman experience is to camp. There are so many cute beach sites to choose from, and some that allow only a few tents each night.

Anchorage Bay.

PLANNING

ACCESS: The Abel Tasman Coast Track is accessible by road in four places. Marahau is 67 kilometres from Nelson and an easy 1.5 hour drive on a sealed road. Wainui Bay is 21 kilometres from Tākaka in Golden Bay and a much further drive from Nelson, with the last 2 kilometres of road being unsealed; Tōtaranui is 32 kilometres from Tākaka, with the last 12 kilometres unsealed. Awaroa is 31 kilometres from Tākaka and the last 12 kilometres of road are rough and unsealed (note, too, there are two fords, which may flood after heavy rain). Also, from the Awaroa car park on the northern side of the estuary, it's another 25 minute walk to the Awaroa hut and campsite on the southern side of the estuary, which must be crossed (check the tides beforehand).

Alternatively, by boat it takes about 1.5 hours to travel between Tōtaranui and Marahau. Overall, the track is well serviced by public transport, including buses and water taxis.

Be sure to time your crossing of the Torrent Bay Estuary.

ACCOMMODATION, FOOD AND EQUIPMENT: Nelson, the closest city and airport, offers numerous accommodation options. If you want to stay closer to the start of the track, try Motueka, or Tākaka in Golden Bay. Nelson is also the best place to buy any equipment you might need. There are lots of places to eat and purchase food in Nelson, Motueka and Tākaka.

WEATHER: The weather in this area tends to be settled, especially when compared to other parts of New Zealand. A week or more of sunny, cloud-free days is not uncommon. Occasionally, Tasman and Golden Bay get storms (usually from the north-west), which can bring intense rainfall and flooding.

TRACK CONDITIONS: The track is undulating, with no long or difficult hill climbs. It is generally well formed and signposted. There are some small sections that may be considered steep or rough underfoot, and at times these can be muddy. A walking pole is recommended, but, in most cases, walking shoes rather than boots should be sufficient, with maybe a pair of jandals for the beach or around camp in the warmer months.

NOTE: There is a compulsory tidal crossing at Awaroa (check a tide chart beforehand) as well as other, optional, estuary crossings at Torrent Bay and Bark Bay where detours may be required at high tide. For this reason, if you're on a tight schedule, it's worth planning your route in advance.

TRACK DESCRIPTION

Marahau to Anchorage: 4 hrs, 12.4 km

The start of the track crosses an estuary over the Marahau causeway with its abundant wading bird life, and then winds easily through open country before reaching a beech forest. Keep an eye out for the many different coastal birds along the beaches, but also on the headlands, marshland areas, offshore islands and even the open water. Keep an eye out for shags on the rocky outcrops, and terns flying their swallow-like lope over the sea. Perhaps a highlight might be catching a glimpse of little blue penguins leaving their burrows on some of the islands at first light, hunting for food in the ocean during the day and then returning to shore at dusk. The first of many beautiful beaches you will pass is Tinline Bay, also the first campsite option. There is a short, signposted nature walk at Tinline Bay (20 minutes return), where you get to look at an odd tree growing in an unlikely place.

Views stretch east over Tasman Bay, with Nelson in the distance and Fisherman Island and then Adele Island much closer, before the track heads inland, passing in and out of several small valleys and emerging into the open again above a stretch of beach that is Anchorage Bay. From here it is a gradual descent to the Anchorage hut and campsite. Note that Anchorage Bay can get particularly busy during the summer holiday period, and it is a very popular option for the traditional New Year's Eve party.

There are a number of other camping options between Marahau and Anchorage: Tinline; Coquille Bay; Apple Tree Bay; Akersten Bay; Watering Cove; Observation Beach; and Te Pukatea Bay.

Anchorage to Bark Bay: 3–4 hrs, 8.4–11.5 km

There are two options for travelling the next section of track: the high-tide track (4 hours, 11.5 km), and the low-tide crossing of the estuary at Torrent Bay, also known as Rākauroa (3 hours, 8.4 km). The estuary can be crossed 2 hours either side of low tide, but be sure to follow the marker poles. You will see that there are still a number of holiday homes in the bay, as it has remained privately owned land, excluded from the Abel Tasman National Park since its formation in 1942. Frenchman Dumont D'Urville sailed here in 1827 on his boat the *Astrolabe*; he mapped the local coastline and named the bay during his exploration of the land. Later, a small quarry was established here, and there was also forestry activity.

Continue walking through a pleasant, forest-cocooned track, eventually coming to a nearly 50 metre-long suspension bridge spanning Falls River. There are some small climbs through this section of track, with occasional intimate views down to various bays and coves, before the track eventually leads back to the sea and the golden sands of Bark Bay.

There is the option of a side trip to Cascade Falls (1.5 hours return), which is a beautifully situated waterfall to cool off on a hot day. Note that the track to the falls is steep in a few places. Another short side trip leads to Cleopatra's Pool, which has a natural rock slide.

There is one campsite before Bark Bay at Torrent Bay, but it is perhaps nicer to carry on to the Bark Bay site.

Bark Bay to Awaroa: 4.5 hrs, 13.5 km

You can cross the Bark Bay Estuary 2 hours either side of low tide, or alternately take the high-tide track, which is only another 10 minutes around the edge of the estuary. A short but steep climb follows, which takes you through more forest stands of various trees including beech and mānuka. Birdsong along this stretch can be quite soothing. Soon enough, though, you will be returning to the coast, at Tonga Quarry, and from there it's only a short section with nice views to Onetahuti Bay – one of the longest and possibly most beautiful beaches in the Abel Tasman National Park, if not all of New Zealand! Take time to enjoy this section of the coast in the knowledge that you are roughly halfway.

Once you feel refreshed, regain the track, which passes over the forested Tonga Saddle before descending to Awaroa Inlet. If the tide is

The suspension bridge spanning Falls River.

full, wait for the water to recede enough for the walk around to the hut or campsite at Awaroa.

If you feel like finishing your walking for the day earlier, there are a number of campsites between Bark Bay and Awaroa: Mosquito Bay; Tonga Quarry; and Onetahuti Bay.

Awaroa to Tōtaranui: 2.5 hrs, 7 km

Awaroa Inlet can be crossed no more than 1.5 hours before or 2 hours after low tide. From here you can either walk to the car park at the road end or continue along the track, alternating between more sandy beaches and rocky headlands, and eventually coming to Tōtaranui (where there is also road access).

Tōtaranui to Whariwharangi Bay: 3 hrs, 10 km

Climb over a scenic headland and continue above Anapai Bay and Mutton Cove, eventually coming to the site of a former homestead

While there is plenty of water traffic, the park still feels intimate and peaceful.

(built around 1896) and the historic Whariwharangi Hut, just above the beach. This area of the track is much quieter than to the south.

There are a number of campsites between Awaroa and Whariwharangi: Waiharakeke Bay; Tōtaranui; Anapai Bay; and Mutton Cove.

Whariwharangi Bay to Wainui Bay: 2 hrs, 6 km

Climb through forest to a saddle that looks over the tranquil Wainui Bay and the end of your journey. The final section of track drops gradually down to the bay, then follows the shoreline of the estuary to the car park and road.

Kayaking

For some people the main attraction of the Abel Tasman National Park is the opportunity to kayak the coastline, rather than walk the track. Whether you do a shorter day-paddle or tackle a full-length, multi-day trip, the perspective from and experience on the water is quite different to that on land.

Another secluded beach.

Much of the track is right next to the coastline.

Please note that sea kayaking presents a completely different range of challenges to walking. If you are not particularly experienced at kayaking or confident with other water pursuits, it is advisable to employ a guide and go on an organised trip. Either way, before you choose to be guided or go for it on your own, have a chat with one of the local kayak operators about the various pros and cons of each option.

While this section of the guidebook covers the basics to consider, you should still get a far more detailed account from a local operator before deciding to book huts or campsites along the track. And, along with the clothing and safety equipment listed at the beginning of this book, other specialised kayak gear to take includes a sprayskirt, paddling jacket (although a good raincoat will suffice), a small bilge pump, a spare paddle (between the whole party), and dry-bags for storage.

Wind direction and strength and the overall sea conditions (including swell size) are major considerations when paddling in open water. Even though the coastline will likely be close, you are still exposed to the elements for hours at a time, and this can greatly increase how long it might take to reach the next beach and campsite. Don't forget, either, the ever-present risk of being tipped out of your kayak! Everyone in your party should know how to self-rescue at sea (solo, as well as using a group raft-up technique), and how to pump water out of the craft after climbing back in. In any case, all kayak rental outfits will insist that at least two people are travelling together on the ocean and that you have some previous sea kayaking experience.

Choosing which direction to travel is also a consideration. While the wind here is predominantly from the west, a strong southerly makes for a particularly slow paddle if you are heading back towards Marahau. Check local maritime weather conditions and, again, talk to a local operator.

It is sensible to be conservative when planning how far you might paddle each day (and therefore which campsites or huts you will need to pre-book each night). If you allow extra time for bad weather, there will be less pressure to reach your next destination, and if you arrive early you can use that extra time to relax or explore further, if the sea state allows. If conditions appear too dangerous, the local DOC rangers will allow you to stay at a different campsite to the one you have booked for safety reasons.

Each morning, before starting out, it is important to reassess the wind strength and sea conditions, as well as how rested you are, before committing to the day's paddling. Ask a local DOC office for an updated weather forecast.

Please note: DOC recommends that no kayaking is done north of Onetahuti Bay. This stretch of coast is remote and can be exposed to particularly strong winds and rough seas, making it far more of a challenge than the rest of the park.

POINTS OF INTEREST

The first people

Māori lived along the Abel Tasman coast gathering kai (food) from the sea, estuaries and forests, and the climate was warm enough that they could grow kūmara on suitable sites. Most of their occupation in this specific area was seasonal, but some sites in the Awaroa Estuary became permanent.

On 18 December 1642, the Dutch explorer Abel Tasman anchored his two ships near Wainui in Mohua (Golden Bay). He was the first European to visit Aotearoa New Zealand, although he never personally set foot on land. Tasman was also the first to interact with Māori here, although this meeting didn't go well. Four sailors were killed in an altercation on the water, and Tasman's crew retaliated by killing a local before departing the area, which Tasman named 'Murderers Bay'.

Bird life and trapping

A concerted trapping programme in parts of the national park has been helping to eradicate pests and encourage more bird life back into the forests. Stoats, ferrets and weasels all prey on birds or their eggs, and possums feed on native vegetation. The Abel Tasman Birdsong Trust was formed in 2007 to help DOC with community-based trapping. You may see traps near the track, especially near Torrent Bay. These are regularly checked by local volunteers, so please don't go near or touch them.

Onetahuti Bay, one of the longest and most beautiful beaches in the park.

The shoreline

The coastline of Abel Tasman is a huge part of what makes this landscape so special. Marine reserves are a great way to help with the rejuvenation of local fauna and flora, and the Tonga Island Marine Reserve (which runs one nautical mile out from Awaroa Head to the headland between Bark Bay and Mosquito Bay) has encouraged the regeneration of a much more vibrant sea life.

OFF THE TRACK

Day boat trips

Abel Tasman National Park has a range of water taxi companies who can drop you off at various places along the track or even just take you sightseeing on the water. You can do part- or full-day trips, combining walking, kayaking and/or scenic cruising. Some companies offer a timetable that allows you to change between vessels. If you only have one day spare and want to do as much of the walk as you can, a good option is to get dropped off at Anchorage, Torrent Bay, Bark Bay or even Onetahuti, depending on your fitness, and still have enough time to hike back to Marahau.

Rock climbing in Golden Bay

If rock climbing is your thing there are a number of great limestone sport (bolted) climbing areas close to Tākaka in Golden Bay. Hangdog Camp is a famous climbers' campsite near the most popular climbing area, Payne's Ford.

Inland Pack Track: 3 days, 41 km

The Inland Pack Track is a much more challenging and remote hike compared to the Abel Tasman Coast Track, passing over hilly and mostly forested country between Marahau and Wainui Bay. You will need to arrange transport back to the start (water taxi is easiest), and although you cannot pre-book huts here, the track doesn't get anywhere near as busy as Abel Tasman. If you are feeling particularly energetic you can link the Inland Pack Track with Abel Tasman for a 5–6 day round trip.

Mount Arthur Track: 1.5 hrs, 4 km

The track from Flora car park to Mt Arthur Hut is a very pleasantly angled and scenic walk, and in good weather it is suitable for most people. The track is around 75 kilometres from Nelson, the final 6 kilometre stretch steep and unsealed. The track passes beneath beech forest and then groves of funky mountain dracophyllum, before reaching the hut at the top of the bushline. If you walk uphill a bit further you will break out onto the edge of an area called the Tablelands, from which there's a great view up to Mt Arthur and out over Tasman Bay. In summer, if you are feeling adventurous, the summit of Mt Arthur is a further 2–3 hours. Just be sure to allow enough time for the descent (the same way) back to your vehicle.

High grasslands cover the middle section of the Heaphy Track.

HEAPHY TRACK

PALMS, GRASSES AND TAKAHĒ

HEAPHY TRACK

PALMS, GRASSES AND TAKAHĒ // 78 KM, 3–6 DAYS

— HIGHLIGHTS

- » Choose between walking or cycling the track.
- » Pass through a land of diversity.
- » Watch out for takahē in the Gouland Downs area.
- » Keep an eye out for the rare and native giant land snail.

THINK ALPINE BASINS of tussocks and grasses waving in the breeze. Imagine rainforests filled with our unique nīkau palms, and the nearby roar of the Tasman Sea – keep an eye out for a rare takahē. This is what it means to travel through New Zealand's second-largest and second-newest national park, the Kahurangi – as the Māori name suggests, a treasured possession. And there is probably no better way to experience the Kahurangi than via the Heaphy Track.

While this land may not be filled with high mountains or wide alpine lakes, it has many other unique features making the Heaphy just as appealing as any of the Great Walks. Indeed, the constantly changing terrain is a large part of the reason for journeying here.

Parts of Kahurangi are believed to have been occupied by Māori since the 1400s. Certainly the upper West Coast region was travelled in search of pounamu (greenstone). The track is named after Charles Heaphy who, in 1846, worked as a draughtsman with the New Zealand Company. He and surveyor Thomas Brunner, accompanied by a Māori guide named Kehu, became the first Europeans to traverse the coastal portion of what has become the current track.

By walking the Heaphy, you are also exploring one of the pathways taken by early Māori seeking their pounamu, and then later the similar trails used by Pākehā searching for gold. Make your own journey either on foot or mountain bike (during certain times of year), enjoying the varied nature of the countryside, scenery and wildlife. After you emerge from forest at either end of the track, the interior grasslands of Gouland Downs are a pleasant

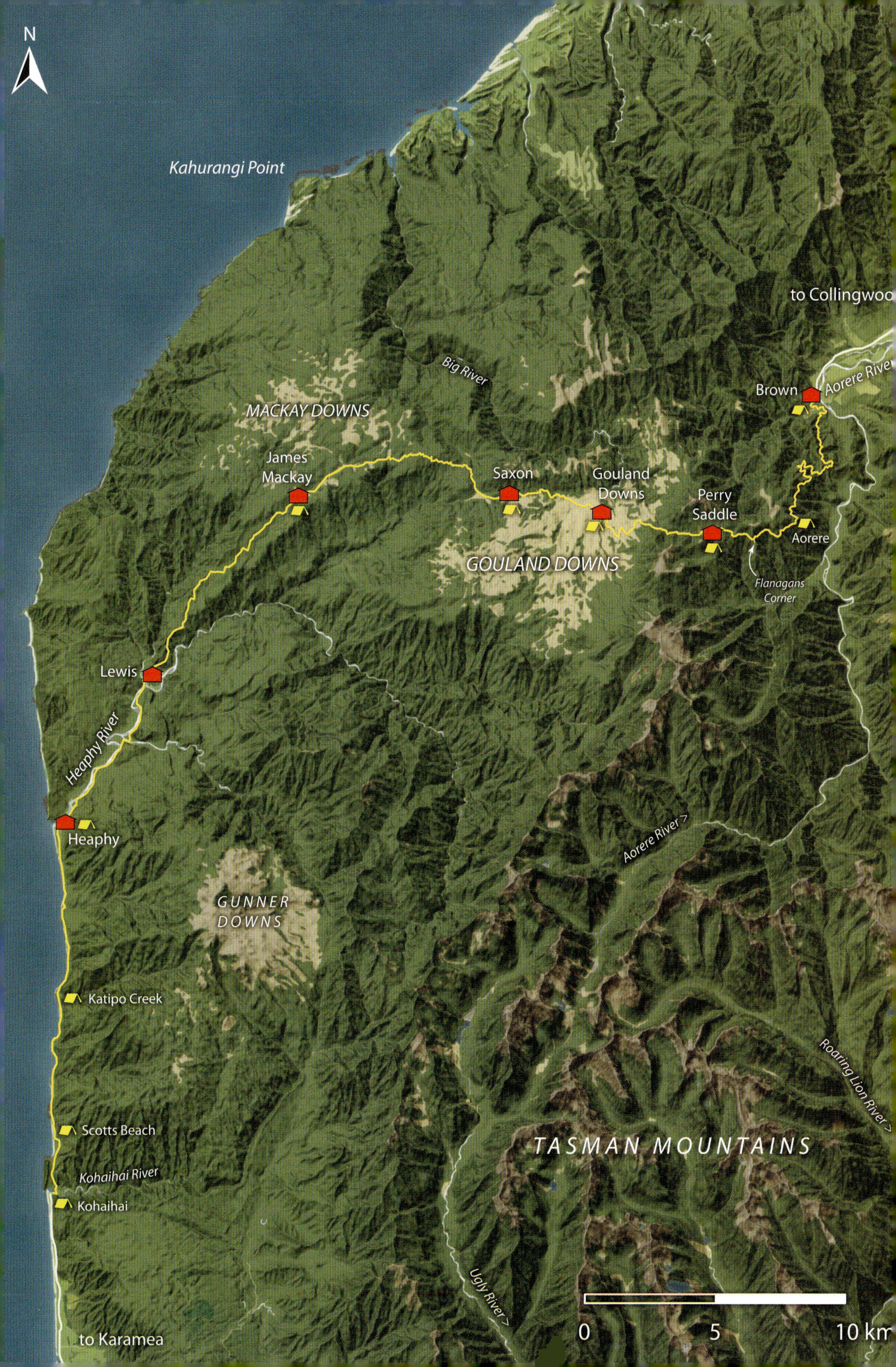

N
Kahurangi Point
to Collingwood
Big River
Aorere River
Brown
MACKAY DOWNS
James Mackay
Saxon
Gouland Downs
Perry Saddle
Aorere
GOULAND DOWNS
Flanagans Corner
Lewis
Heaphy River
Heaphy
Aorere River >
GUNNER DOWNS
Katipo Creek
Roaring Lion River >
Scotts Beach
TASMAN MOUNTAINS
Kohaihai River
Kohaihai
Ugly River >
0
5
10 km
to Karamea

surprise and, for many, the highlight of the trip. The basin of the downs is held in a cusp of mountains to the north, while to the south stretches the largely untracked wilds of the remote interior of Kahurangi National Park. The Arthur Range marks the eastern border of the park, protecting much of the north-west corner of the South Island.

Due to its often temperate climate and slightly lower altitude when compared to the other alpine Great Walks, the Heaphy can usually be walked all year round. Winter is a cool but still pleasant time to explore when the crowds of summer have left and most of the sandflies take their holidays. Also, while there is a steady climb on one of the days, regardless of which direction you walk or bike the track, the altitude gain is less pronounced or taxing than on some of the other Great Walks. Therefore the Heaphy is a good introduction to our alpine lands.

TRACK DETAILS

LOCATION: Kahurangi National Park, north-west Nelson

TRACK TYPE: This is a through track that can be walked or cycled (during the mountain biking season) in either direction.

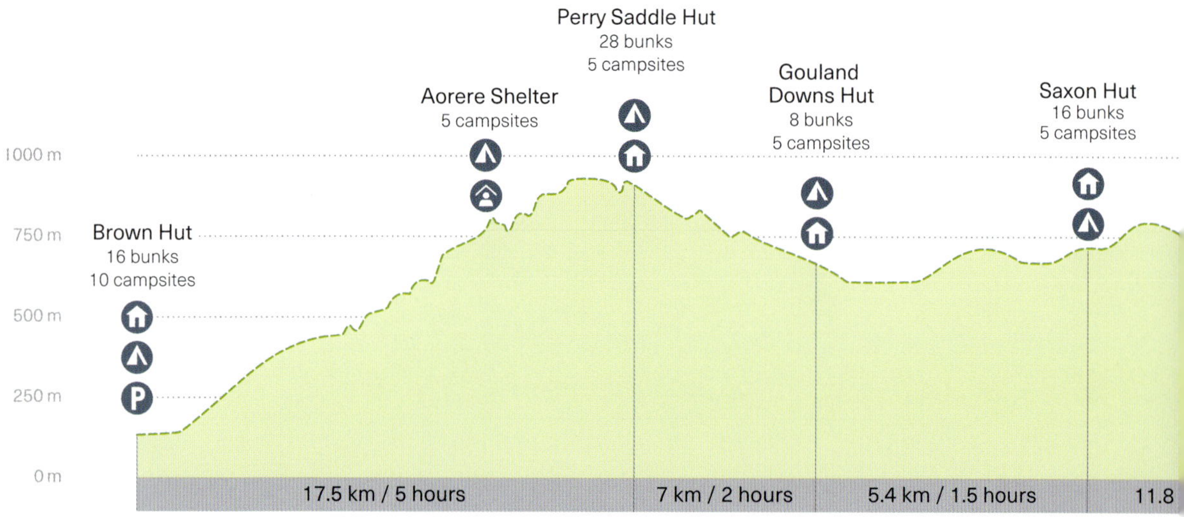

START POINT: Aorere Valley, Golden Bay
END POINT: Kohaihai, West Coast
DISTANCE: 78 km
TIME: 3–6 days walking or 2–4 days mountain biking
SEASON: All year (currently, mountain biking is allowed between 1 May and 30 November)
GRADING: Moderate
DOC HUTS: Brown (16 bunks), Perry Saddle (28 bunks), Gouland Downs (8 bunks), Saxon (16 bunks), James Mackay (28 bunks), Lewis (20 bunks), Heaphy (32 bunks)
DOC CAMPSITES: Brown (10 sites), Aorere Shelter (5 sites), Perry Saddle (5 sites), Gouland Downs (5 sites), Saxon (5 sites), James Mackay (4 sites), Heaphy (20 sites), Katipo Creek Shelter (5 sites), Scotts Beach (10 sites), Kohaihai (50 sites).

RECOMMENDED TRIP OPTION: Both the Golden Bay and Karamea ends of the tracks are unique pockets of New Zealand and worth staying at and exploring before or after doing the track. The recommended direction for the track is Aorere to Kohaihai and, if walking, staying at Perry Saddle, Saxon, James Mackay and Heaphy huts. On bike, you could do the trip in 2 days, staying at either Saxon or James Mackay. For a more relaxed ride add in another night at either Perry Saddle or Heaphy.

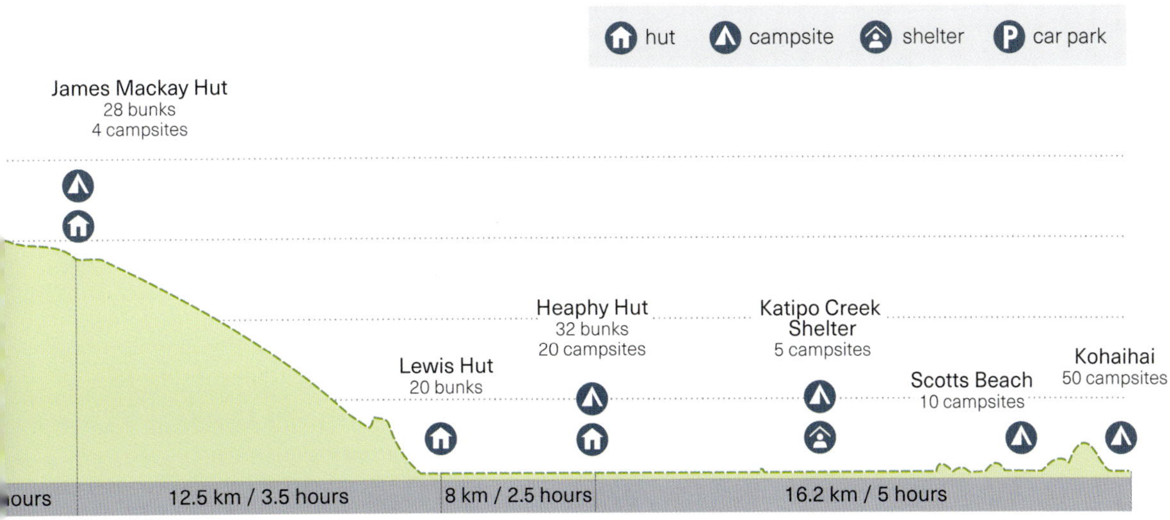

PLANNING

ACCESS: Getting to the start and from the end of the Heaphy Track is the first thing to consider. Brown Hut, which marks the beginning of the track in Golden Bay, and Kohaihai at the finish on the West Coast are around 460 kilometres apart by road. A popular option is to walk the track one way and book a return flight with local operators based in either Tākaka or Karamea.

The start of the track in the Aorere Valley is around 160 kilometres, or 2.5 hours' driving, from Nelson. Kohaihai is 110 kilometres, or almost two hours' driving, from Westport. The closest regional airport is Nelson, and there are regular buses linking Nelson and Westport as well as a number of services that can get you to either end of the track from the closest towns. Telephones at both ends of the track can be used to make a free local call.

ACCOMMODATION, FOOD AND EQUIPMENT: The nearest town in Golden Bay is Tākaka (there is also accommodation even closer at Collingwood), while the city of Nelson is also within reach. On the West Coast, the nearest accommodation is at Karamea, with Westport the closest major town. There is a supermarket in Tākaka and places to eat, while in Karamea there a few places to eat. Nelson has the best selection of outdoor and biking shops.

WEATHER: The weather can vary greatly between Golden Bay and the West Coast. While the northern side of the track may be sheltered, the western side could be much wetter and windier. With this in mind, it pays to take the appropriate clothing for any changes in weather. There is the possibility of snow from Perry Saddle Hut and across the open country of Gouland Downs during winter. Also, some areas of the track are prone to flooding during and after heavy rain (these areas are highlighted in the track description).

TRACK CONDITIONS: The Heaphy Track is well marked and signposted and mostly very easy to follow. But note that some sections may be steep and rough and could be muddy, especially after heavy rain. All of the major stream and river crossings are bridged, and recently there has been a considerable upgrading of the track surface, especially across Gouland Downs, due to the extra usage from cyclists.

TRACK DESCRIPTION

Brown Hut to Perry Saddle Hut: 5 hrs, 17.5 km

The first day is the toughest, with a long, gradual climb up through the beech forest. This route was once surveyed for a road (which explains the mostly gentle angle), and there are opportunities to mark your progress with glimpses out over the Aorere Valley to your left. If it's hot, use the opportunity to refill your water bottle at any stream crossing because it might take you around four hours to reach Aorere Shelter (where there is also a campsite).

From the shelter, the track carries on uphill for another hour or so before reaching the highest point at just over 900 metres altitude. If you feel like another break, look for a short track off to the left that leads to a cool viewpoint at a spot called Flanagans Corner. Back on the main track, the angle eases considerably as you traverse through more forest for another half-hour or so to finally reach the nicely situated Perry Saddle Hut (at around 880 m altitude).

Perry Saddle Hut.

The track passes by a number of rivers.

Saxon Hut.

Perry Saddle Hut to Saxon Hut: 3–4 hrs, 12.5 km

Relax in the knowledge that the hardest yards are now done. From Perry Saddle Hut, the track follows a terrace above Perry Creek through a mixture of forest and clearings of tussock. Soon you will reach the wide country of Gouland Downs, allowing great views out to the west (see if you can spot the track in the distance). This mostly untouched landscape is a remnant of an earlier New Zealand. Over time the downs became eroded to a nearly flat surface known as a peneplain; some of the rocks here are 500 million years old, making them among the oldest found in New Zealand.

You'll come to a pole on the side of the track with lots of old tramping boots on it, and, not long after that, the historical Gouland Downs Hut. Some people choose to spend the night here, and there are limestone formations nearby that are worth exploring. But it's not that far across mostly flat, open grasslands to the newer Saxon Hut. It pays to stick to the track here, as you can get rather disoriented in such a featureless landscape, especially in low cloud. Note that the Saxon Hut area is probably the best place to perhaps see a takahē.

Saxon Hut to James Mackay Hut: 3 hrs, 12 km

This is a pretty easy day's travel between the two huts, allowing plenty of time to explore and enjoy the landscape. From Saxon Hut, cross more wide

The view from James Mackay Hut.

tussock fields and some pockets of beech forest along the way, with a few gradual ups and downs – especially between Gouland Downs and Mackay Downs. Be aware that a section of the track on Mackay Downs can flood in extremely wet conditions, sometimes becoming impassable and quite dangerous. There are marker poles through these sections to indicate where the track goes. If this area is too flooded to safely continue, you are advised to return to Saxon Hut and wait for the water to recede.

As you approach James Mackay Hut, you will get a view down towards the distant Heaphy River and the Tasman Sea. The hut is just a few minutes' walk above the track on an open terrace, and has great views from its deck and windows.

James Mackay Hut to Heaphy Hut: 5–6 hrs, 20 km

This is the longest day on the track, but the first portion is an easy descent to the Heaphy River through beech forest and then the lusher, more layered West Coast podocarp forest. You will come to Lewis Hut after about 3 hours, which is a good place to stop for lunch, and some may choose to spend the night here. Soon after, cross a 150 metre suspension bridge over the Heaphy River, its waters stained brown by natural tannins. The track now continues along the true left bank of the river through a beautifully dense forest of towering kahikatea, rimu and rātā.

Nīkau palms become more prevalent the closer you get to the mouth of the Heaphy and the West Coast. The coastline has a rugged, windswept beauty, and not surprisingly the wind and rain here can be full-on during a storm. (Note that parts of this track can flood during periods of heavy rain.) The mouth of the Heaphy is also the junction of two historic pounamu trails, with archaeological exploration uncovering evidence of occupation by Māori dating back 500 years.

Be aware that it is extremely dangerous going for a swim or even a wade in the mouth of the Heaphy River because of the rips and strong tidal currents.

Heaphy Hut to Kohaihai River Mouth: 4–6 hrs, 16 km

The final day takes you south along the coast, where the ocean meets the forest. This is a stunning and unique part of New Zealand, but keep an eye out for large wave surges during high tides, which can make the track impassable until the tide drops again. The track south to Kohaihai passes mostly beneath the forest canopy, but in some places, if the tide is low, you can instead walk along the beach. There is a final climb over Kohaihai Saddle and then a descent to the Kohaihai River and car park.

Mountain biking

Along with walking, the Heaphy Track is a great multi-day mountain bike adventure. It does get biked in a single day, but for a much more enjoyable (and less taxing) experience you are advised to take 2 or 3. Regardless of which direction you choose there will be one day of solid uphill riding. And, as with walking, you are advised to start at Brown Hut.

Note that this ride is quite a step up from, say, the Central Otago Rail Trail or the Queen Charlotte Track in Marlborough Sounds. The terrain is technical in places, the weather potentially much worse, and you will need to be completely self-sufficient in terms of dealing with mechanical breakdowns. You will want to have a reliable bike and a reasonable standard of fitness (including being comfortable spending up to six hours in the saddle each day), and you will of course be carrying all of your own food, clothes, overnight and personal gear, as well as bike tools and equipment.

For the 2 day option, riders choose to stay at either Saxon Hut or James

Hikers and mountain bikers share the track during certain times of the year.

Mackay Hut. For the easier 3 day ride, plan to spend a night at Perry Saddle and then Heaphy Hut. In terms of organising transport from the end of the track afterwards, note that some of the local aircraft between Golden Bay and Karamea have bike attachments on the undersides of their wings!

Because this is a shared track, some mountain-biking etiquette – otherwise known as common sense – is required.

- Don't ride too fast. There is the possibility of a walker or another rider at any stage.
- Stick to the track. Riding bikes off the track will increase erosion considerably.
- Keep your bikes out of the huts and off the decks. Bike stands are generally provided.
- Don't be a liability to other riders. That means taking everything you might need to fix your bike if it breaks down.

POINTS OF INTEREST

The wildlife

Kahurangi National Park hosts more than half of New Zealand's native plant species and over 80 per cent of its alpine plant species. This means the flora within the park boundary is the most diverse found in any of our national parks. There is also plenty of fauna. Along with the takahē, which you may be lucky enough to meet during your journey, you may also spot or hear the tūī, bellbird, kererū and robin. Two of our native parrots, the kea and kākā, are also found in the park, as well as the whio (rare blue duck).

The long-tailed bat and rarer short-tailed bat were this country's only land mammals before the arrival of people and their animal entourage. If you are lucky during your walk you may catch sight of some around dusk as they come out into the open to feed on insects.

A second mainland site for takahē

In 2018, New Zealand's rare flightless bird, the takahē, was released back into Kahurangi National Park. Complementing a successful wild population based in the remote Murchison Mountains of Fiordland, this release site in Gouland Downs is much more accessible to most New Zealanders.

Spot the great spotted kiwi

Kahurangi National Park is home to the great spotted kiwi or roroa. On the track, the birds are mostly around Gouland Downs, and you may hear them calling at night from the Perry Saddle, Gouland Downs and Saxon huts. The roroa is a little larger than the North Island brown kiwi, with mottled or spotted plumage.

Various species of kiwi were once widespread throughout New Zealand, evolving to a life on forest floors that were largely free of natural predators. But when Māori and then Europeans arrived with their various mammals – including rats, dogs, cats, and stoats and other mustelids – the kiwi, especially its vulnerable chicks, had few defences against them. Today, the roroa is found in the upper South Island as well as Arthur's Pass, and there is also a small population in the Rotoiti Mainland Island Reserve in Nelson Lakes National Park.

Crossing the Heaphy River.

OFF THE TRACK

Karamea and Golden Bay are both fantastic areas to explore before or after you have walked or ridden the Heaphy Track.

Karamea

Take an interesting drive north from Westport until you almost reach the end of the road (and the finish of the Heaphy Track). Nestled between the mountains of the Southern Alps and the wildness of the Tasman Sea, Karamea is a largely unspoilt and unique pocket of New Zealand. There are some small areas of farmland and forestry nearby, but most of this community of around 600 residents is surrounded by the Kahurangi National Park.

There are cool places to stay in the town and heaps of things to do,

The coastal section is filled with
the unmistakable nīkau palms.

including heli-rafting the impressive Karamea River (a thoroughly recommended adventure!), surfing one of the local, uncrowded breaks, taking a tour of the Honeycomb caves and arches in the Oparara Basin, or exploring the other local walks and bike rides.

Golden Bay

Golden Bay is probably most well known because of the 26 kilometre finger of sand known as Farewell Spit. New Zealand's longest sandspit is certainly worth exploring, as is the windy gravel road to the Anatoki River mouth on the West Coast. This is about as remote an area as you can drive to in the South Island.

Golden Bay itself, also known as Mohua, is a curving bay of mostly shallow water, and the resting area for migrating whales and dolphins, such as southern right whales, humpback whales and possibly also pygmy blue whales. In summer it is popular with fishers and holidaymakers, with the local town, Tākaka, offering accommodation and eateries. A few minutes' drive from Tākaka is Te Waikoropupū Springs – New Zealand's largest freshwater springs, source of reputedly the clearest spring water in the world. Payne's Ford is a local and very popular rock-climbing area.

Enjoy walking along the beach during the final day to Kohaihai.

Limestone cliffs rise above the Pororari River.

PAPAROA TRACK

THE ENDLESS SUNSET

PAPAROA TRACK

THE ENDLESS SUNSET // 55 KM, 2–4 DAYS

— HIGHLIGHTS

- Travel from the heart of the South Island over a mountain range to the coast.
- Explore the edge of a rugged, mostly untracked landscape.
- Watch out for weka along sides of the track.
- Enjoy the mix of open alpine country, dense forest and a picturesque river gorge.
- Walk beneath towering limestone cliffs.
- Learn about the area's extensive – and tragic – mining history.

WELCOME TO THE newest Great Walk: the first to be added in 25 years, and one that can be walked or biked all year round. Set on the stunning West Coast of the South Island, the recently completed Paparoa Great Walk crosses both the Paparoa National Park and the Paparoa Range.

The West Coast is tough. For some, it's an intimidating environment. While at first glance it may not seem as dramatic as other higher, more mountainous areas, the region has a history of offering unrelenting challenge, sometimes with tragic results. Even today, civilisation has chiselled only a few pathways into and through the landscape. And the wind, the rain, the forest and the ocean are always trying to claim those pathways back.

Tracks and roads act as corridors between the local settlements and places of work or areas of recognised beauty. The Great Coast Road, which leads travellers from Westport south to Greymouth, has been described as one of the top ten coastal drives in the world, and for good reason. Do not be surprised if you have to stop at one of the many viewpoints, especially at sunset, unable to continue your journey until all light has left the horizon.

The Paparoa Great Walk weaves through the heart of this country. It starts near the historically rich interior around Blackball, a small town 30 kilometres inland from Greymouth. Blackball was named after the Blackball Shipping Line, which originally leased nearby land to mine for

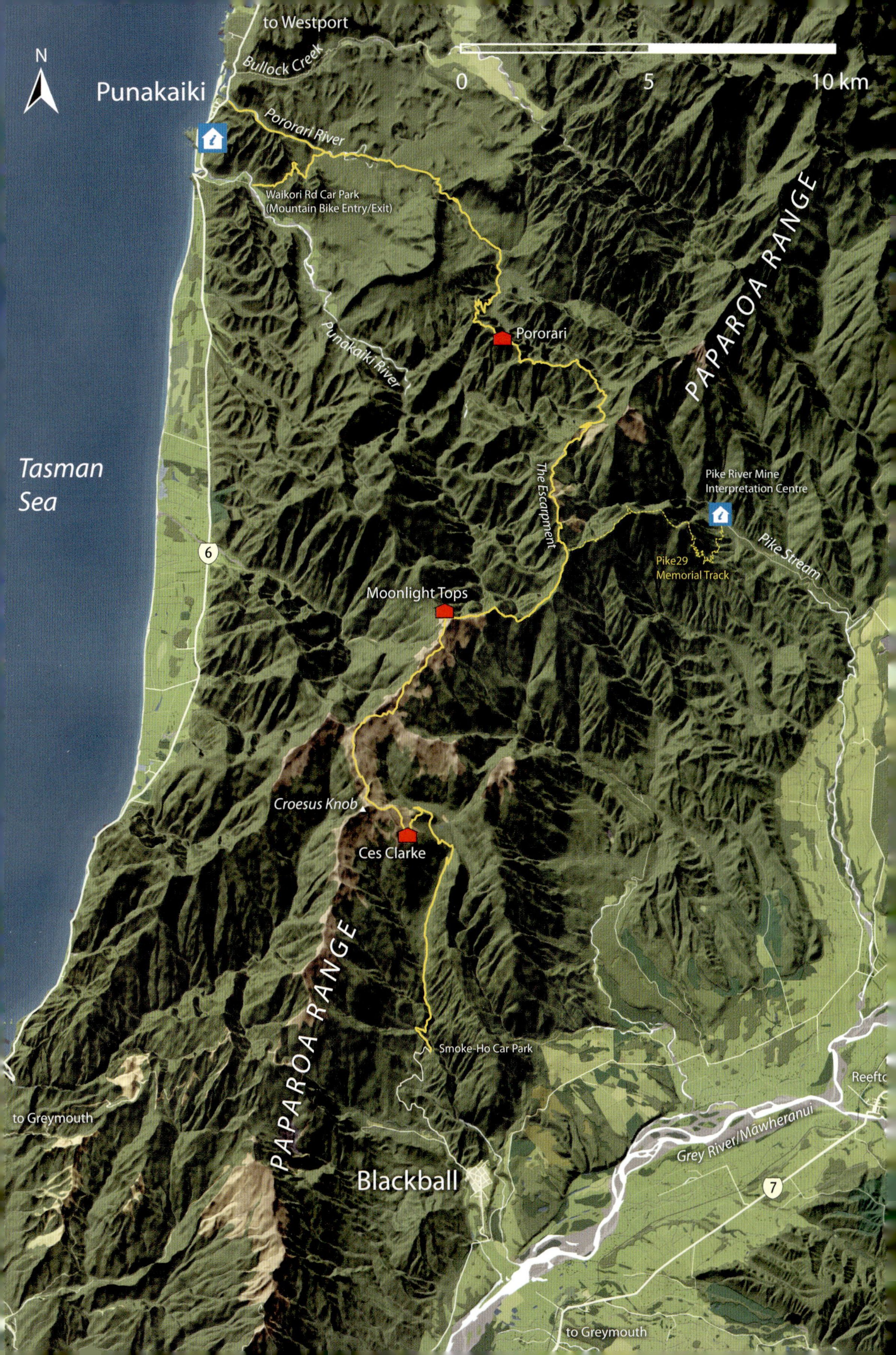

N
to Westport
Bullock Creek
0
5
10 km
Punakaiki
Pororari River
Waikori Rd Car Park
(Mountain Bike Entry/Exit)
Pororari
PAPAROA RANGE
Punakaiki River
Tasman
Sea
The Escarpment
Pike River Mine
Interpretation Centre
Pike Stream
Pike29
Memorial Track
6
Moonlight Tops
Croesus Knob
Ces Clarke
PAPAROA RANGE
Smoke-Ho Car Park
to Greymouth
Grey River/Māwheranui
7
Blackball
to Greymouth

coal. These days Blackball is recognised more for its characterful hotel, formerly known as the Blackball Hilton (and a court case over naming rights with its more famous namesake), as well as its tasty local sausages and salami. Blackball is also the closest community to the site of the recent Pike River mining disaster.

From Blackball, the walk climbs up over the Paparoa Range – the backbone of Paparoa National Park – and then down into a limestone cliff-lined river gorge that leads to Punakaiki and the coast.

There are views on the alpine tops that will stop you in your tracks, and stands of trees so dense that you might wonder if you have gone back in time. Step even a few metres off the trail and all sense of direction can easily be lost. Sounds are swallowed by the thickness of the forest and the clinging undergrowth. Yes, this is rugged country, and it can quickly remind you of your limits if you don't pay it enough respect.

As you travel, keep a cautious eye out for a particularly nosy, flightless bird – the ubiquitous weka. Don't be surprised if it tries to steal your lunch, or even your watch!

While the bedrock of the Paparoa Range was formed from granite, most of the rock you can see is limestone. The unusual shapes – including the coastal stacks that make up the famous Pancake Rocks tourist attraction at Punakaiki – have come about because limestone is water-permeable (and the rainfall here is notoriously high). This also means there are hidden caves and sink holes throughout the park. It's another reason to be sure to stay on the track!

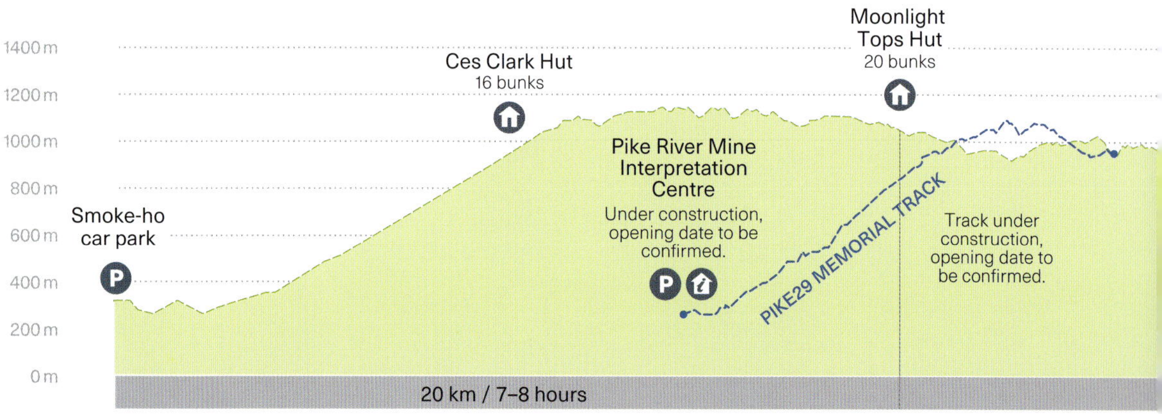

Your starting point for the track: the infamous Blackball Hilton. A great place to spend the night, or at least stop for a coffee or a beer, before starting the track.

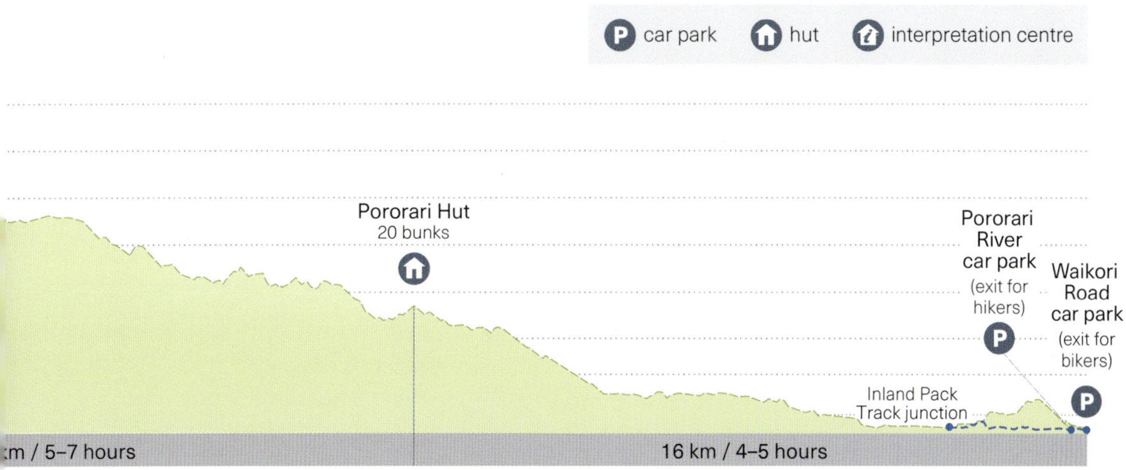

From the Smoke-ho car park, the first part of the track involves a steady climb through beech and podocarp forest.

TRACK DETAILS

LOCATION: Greymouth, Westland

TRACK TYPE: This is a through trip that can be walked or cycled in either direction, starting from Punakaiki or Blackball. The track is purpose-built to be dual use all year round. There are steady climbs involved on the first day regardless of which direction you choose, but generally the terrain is undulating and easy underfoot. Note that the Blackball end (including part of the historic Croesus Track), although mostly easily angled, is considerably rougher terrain for biking than the rest of the track. The following track details are written for walkers starting from Blackball.

START POINT: Smoke-ho car park (8 km from Blackball)
END POINT: Punakaiki
DISTANCE: 55 km
TIME: 2–4 days approx
SEASON: Any time of year due to the area's more temperate climate

(compared to some other parts of the South Island at least!) Note that rainfall is high, and the alpine tops are very exposed to wind.

GRADING: Moderate fitness required

DOC HUTS: Ces Clark (16 bunks), Moonlight Tops (20 bunks), Pororari (20 bunks)

DOC CAMPSITES: None

RECOMMENDED TRIP OPTION: If you are walking, begin from the Blackball end (you will need transport to the track start at Smoke-ho car park) and finish along the Pororari River Track at Punakaiki. (Cyclists starting at Blackball will finish at the Punakaiki River Track.) This is a comfortable 3 day tramp, although it can be stretched to 4 if you add a night at Ces Clark Hut.

For bikers, it is advisable to ride in the other direction. The gradient from Punakaiki up to and beyond Pororari Hut is more gentle, with a track surface of a better standard, and the rougher part of the track at the Blackball end is more easily negotiated descending. If you go up from the Blackball end you will likely be pushing your bike a lot.

PLANNING

ACCESS: Travel to either end of the Paparoa Track is straightforward, and it's an easy hour's drive from the start to the finish. Greymouth is the nearest major settlement, but Punakaiki and Blackball are much closer. Both communities are unique, have other nearby attractions, and are worth spending time getting to know. There are local operators who can transport you or your vehicle to either end of the track.

ACCOMMODATION, FOOD AND EQUIPMENT: Greymouth has everything you will need to stock up on before starting your trip. Blackball and Punakaiki have decent accommodation and options for eating out, but little else in terms of supplies. There is also a DOC visitor centre at Punakaiki.

WEATHER: The West Coast climate is considered mild, especially in the

Ces Clark Hut is an ideal place to stop for lunch, or even for the night.

Pororari Hut offers views over the surrounding country as well as out towards Punakaiki on the West Coast.

Greymouth region and to the north. Summer here tends not to be too hot, nor winter too cold. The average annual rainfall in this area is around 2.5 metres, so a good raincoat is essential.

TRACK CONDITIONS: The Paparoa Track has been specifically constructed as a Great Walk, and offers all-year use for both walkers and mountain bikers. Most of the track is built to a high standard, with a stable and mostly even surface, and with swing bridges across all of the major waterways. Note that it also incorporates some existing tracks, including a section of the Croesus Track, an old miners' route over the Paparoa Range. Parts of the Croesus Track, while a steady gradient, are nonetheless quite rough, with sections of mud and slippery boulders. Mountain bikers in particular need to be careful travelling through this section.

TRACK DESCRIPTION

Smoke-ho car park to Moonlight Tops Hut: 7 hrs, 20 km

The first day is the roughest underfoot as it incorporates part of the old Croesus Track. A few ups and downs take you through a dense forest of beech and podocarps before a gradual, constant ascent towards Ces Clark Hut. As you make this climb for 'enjoyment', spare a thought for the goldminers who used to have to cross here for work. There are still mining relics to be found along parts of the track.

As you break free of the forest and out onto the alpine tops of grass and tussock, no doubt with tired legs from all of the altitude gain, be comforted by the knowledge that you are only a few minutes from Ces Clark Hut (approximately 4 hours from Smoke-ho). This is a great place to rest and have lunch, or even spend your first night if you want to take 4 days to complete the walk. Just above the hut, there is also the option of taking a short detour up to Croesus Knob, the highest point on the track at 1200 metres (about 10 minutes one way from the turn-off).

You are now roughly halfway to Moonlight Tops Hut. Continue along the open tops, passing the junction where the Croesus Track splits, passes Mt Ryall and descends to Barrytown. The Grey River is far below you to

The track continues through the forest above the Pororari River.

the south-east, and the great expanse of the Tasman Sea stretches west to the horizon. But, on a clear day, it's the unobstructed view of the Southern Alps all the way to Aoraki/Mount Cook – our highest mountain – in the south that is perhaps most compelling. This is a special sight from such a perspective, one usually reserved for mountain climbers and high-altitude trampers, and a graphic illustration of how the Main Divide has formed in almost a straight line along the fault line of the Indo-Australian and Pacific tectonic plates.

The modern, and superbly located, Moonlight Tops Hut is a perfect place to rest and absorb the views in any direction while the sun slips beyond the ocean.

Note that half of this day is spent in an open and exposed alpine environment. Wind and driving rain (and, very occasionally, snow) can dramatically change conditions in a short period of time. Be sure to manage your own safety. If you aren't sure about continuing because of overly challenging conditions – especially if you or anyone in your group should get too cold – make the decision early to turn around.

Moonlight Tops Hut to Pororari Hut: 6 hrs, 19 km

Head off this morning fully rested and with the knowledge that nearly all of the uphill is behind you. Enjoy gradual undulations across the alpine tops, passing first a junction with the Moonlight Track that descends back towards Blackball, and then later the Pike29 Memorial Track (under construction at time of writing). Take in the continuing views, mostly of a landscape that's had very little human impact, before eventually entering forest again. The warped, stunted trees you pass beneath have grown that way because of the prevailing wind and the harsh environment.

Being newly constructed, the track here is much easier underfoot, especially when compared to the previous day. As you traverse closer to Pororari Hut, the podocarp forest becomes more dense (and not so warped). Far below to your left can be seen the upper reaches of the Punakaiki River, while to the right is Tindale Creek. This watershed drains into the Pororari River and you will follow it the rest of the way out to the coast on your last day.

There is a final short climb up to Pororari Hut, but the effort is worth it. The hut is set on an open knoll with a clear view of the coast at Punakaiki – another great spot to watch the sunset.

Pororari Hut to Punakaiki: 5 hrs, 16 km

There is a steady, gradual descent from Pororari Hut towards the Pororari River and lower country that leads to the west. This part of the track is also mostly new and makes for pleasant going. It continues above the banks of the Pororari River, crossing the river a number of times and offering glimpses of the impressive, towering limestone cliffs as you draw closer to the coast. Beside you, the river increases in size as more side streams enter it. There are areas of dense, quiet forest and more open sections of regrowth, with nīkau palms becoming more prevalent.

Stopping to take a rest in a quiet and seemingly uninhabited part of the track, don't be surprised if a bush nearby suddenly rustles. A small, pointy-nosed, brown feathered head may soon appear, shortly followed by the body of an inquisitive and quite untrustworthy stumpy brown bird. Weka are well known for their curiosity and their keenness to swipe anything shiny and unattended. You have been warned.

Towards the end of your journey you will pass the turn-off to the Inland Pack Track, and later a junction with the Pororari River Track. Walkers follow this track, continuing along the banks of the Pororari River to Punakaiki, while cyclists take the alternative track, up over a final climb to join the Punakaiki River just before it reaches the sea.

Mountain biking

Just like the Heaphy Track, the Paparoa Track is a great 2 day mountain bike adventure. (Although it can be biked in 1 day, you are advised to allow plenty of time and take 2.) Regardless of which direction you choose to take, the first day will include a fair amount of uphill riding (given the highest point of the track is well over 1000 metres above sea level).

Note that this ride is quite a step up from the Central Otago Rail Trail and the Queen Charlotte Track in Marlborough Sounds (and around the same grade as the Heaphy). The terrain is technical in places, the weather potentially much worse (especially on the open tops), and you will need to be completely self-sufficient in dealing with mechanical breakdowns. You will want to have a reasonable standard of fitness (including being comfortable spending up to six hours in the saddle each day) and a reliable bike, and you must carry all of your own food, clothes, and overnight and personal gear, as well as bike tools and equipment.

For the 2 day option it is best to stay at either Moonlight Tops or Pororari Hut. Another option (if you want to avoid the rougher Croesus Track section, and if hut bookings are high at Moonlight Tops and Pororari) is to ride through to Ces Clark and stay the night there, returning to Punakaiki the next day.

Because this is a shared track, some mountain biking etiquette – otherwise known as common sense – is required. The future of mountain biking in our national parks depends largely on mountain bikers being respectful and showing courtesy towards walkers.

Don't ride too fast, especially if you can't see very far ahead of you. There is the possibility of a walker or another rider at any stage.

Stick to the track. Riding bikes off the track will increase erosion considerably.

Swing bridges make crossing the many side streams easy.

Keep your bikes out of the huts and off the decks. Bike stands have usually been provided.

Make conservative decisions about your own safety. There are sections of the track that are quite exposed, both to the wind and to steep drop-offs. Get off and walk if you aren't sure.

Don't be a liability to other riders. That means taking everything you might need to fix your bike if it breaks down.

POINTS OF INTEREST

Blackball and Punakaiki

The contrast between the two ends of the track couldn't be greater, and the ongoing changes in the two settlements couldn't be more interesting. Call it a microcosm of New Zealand's small communities.

Punakaiki is already a tourist hub, small but often busy, with the Pancake

Rocks being one of the main attractions on the West Coast. Locals and those who work here are used to dealing with visitors, so the inclusion of a Great Walk won't likely be too much of a change for them.

Blackball is entirely different. Off the beaten track, historically it has attracted far fewer visitors and the locals are used to keeping to themselves. But, obviously, with a new tourist attraction nearby this will change.

Managing local interests

Given that this is the first Great Walk in 25 years, and one that has been purpose-built, juggling the various vested interests is an intriguing challenge, to say the least. Along with the various impacts on the two main communities affected, there is also the issue of managing track usage and how that affects the experience. Having huts on a multi-day hike is a natural way to limit numbers; there are only so many bunks. But questions around

The track continues along a bank just above the Pororari River, eventually meeting a junction with the Inland Pack Track.

ventures like heli-biking, where clients can be dropped at a specified location and bike out in a day, need to be well considered and monitored.

There are other local commercial factors, too. Only part of the Paparoa Great Walk is within the Paparoa National Park. Land outside the park has been mined for decades, historically for gold but more recently for coal. Mining has been one of the main employers on the West Coast, but as an industry (especially coal) it clashes with the principles of protectionism around a national park. Hence, conflicting views between local miners and conservationists have created friction in the communities.

Paparoa Wildlife Trust

Like any natural environment worth preserving, the Paparoa National Park has its champions. The Paparoa Wildlife Trust has been working diligently with DOC to set up and manage conservation projects in the southern

What better way to celebrate the end of the track at Punakaiki than to watch the sun descend over the Tasman Sea.

The Paparoa Track ends at the spectacular coastline of Punakaiki.

region of the Paparoa Range. Trapping programmes to protect local whio (blue duck) and roroa (great spotted kiwi) from introduced predators such as stoats have helped these local populations stabilise.

OFF THE TRACK

Moonlight Track

This is a good 1 or 2 day alternative, starting and finishing at Blackball. Ride the first part of the Paparoa Great Walk (staying at either Ces Clark or Moonlight Tops if you prefer), and then take the turn-off just past Moonlight Tops Hut. While it's all downhill from here, note there will be some pushing involved as the track is very challenging in places.

Pike29 Memorial Track

Much has been publicised about the terrible tragedy at the Pike River Mine, where 29 miners were killed in 2010. The mine site and land surrounding it has been incorporated into the Paparoa National Park. The Pike29 Memorial Track will honour those men from the local community who lost their lives. The track, nearly 11 kilometres each way, can be accessed independently from Blackball or as a side trip off the Paparoa Great Walk. There are also plans for an interpretation centre at the Pike River Mine site.

Inland Pack Track

The 25 kilometre (one way), 2–3 day track is one of the more challenging in the region, and certainly a step up from the Paparoa Great Walk. Branching off from near the Punakaiki end of the Paparoa Great Walk, the track has camping sites rather than huts and goes from Punakaiki to Fox River in

Moonlight Tops Hut.

On the tops between Ces Clark Hut and Moonlight Tops Hut.

the north. One camping site is the impressive Ballroom Overhang – a large limestone feature. The track was initially built back in the 1860s as a safer option than what used to be very rugged travel along the coast.

Be sure to check with DOC at Punakaiki to gather information and discuss suitability before committing to this track. And because part of it traverses along and often through a river, do not attempt it if water levels are high.

Croesus Track

This old miners' track crosses the southern Paparoa Range between Barrytown, north of Greymouth, and Blackball in the Grey Valley. It's 18 kilometres long and can be hiked in 2 days (staying at Ces Clark Hut) or 1 really long day. Recently, it has also become popular with mountain bikers (although there is a lot of carrying or pushing your bike required). For a shorter option, hike for an hour or so up from Barrytown to enjoy the ancient forest and the views over the Tasman Sea. The local hotel at

Barrytown is well worth stopping at before or afterwards for a coffee, a beer or a meal.

Point Elizabeth Walkway

Here's another track, but at 5.5 kilometres (one way) it's much shorter, easier and closer to Greymouth. Start at either Cobden or Rapahoe and follow a gravel coastal walk through the forest of nīkau palms and mamaku (black tree fern) entwined with supplejack vines and kiekie. There are also large podocarps such as rimu, kahikatea and miro, along with the northern rātā and its crimson flowers during spring and summer. You are never far from the sea, and often accompanied by the sound of huge waves crashing against the land.

ROUTEBURN TRACK

THE TALE OF TWO PARKS

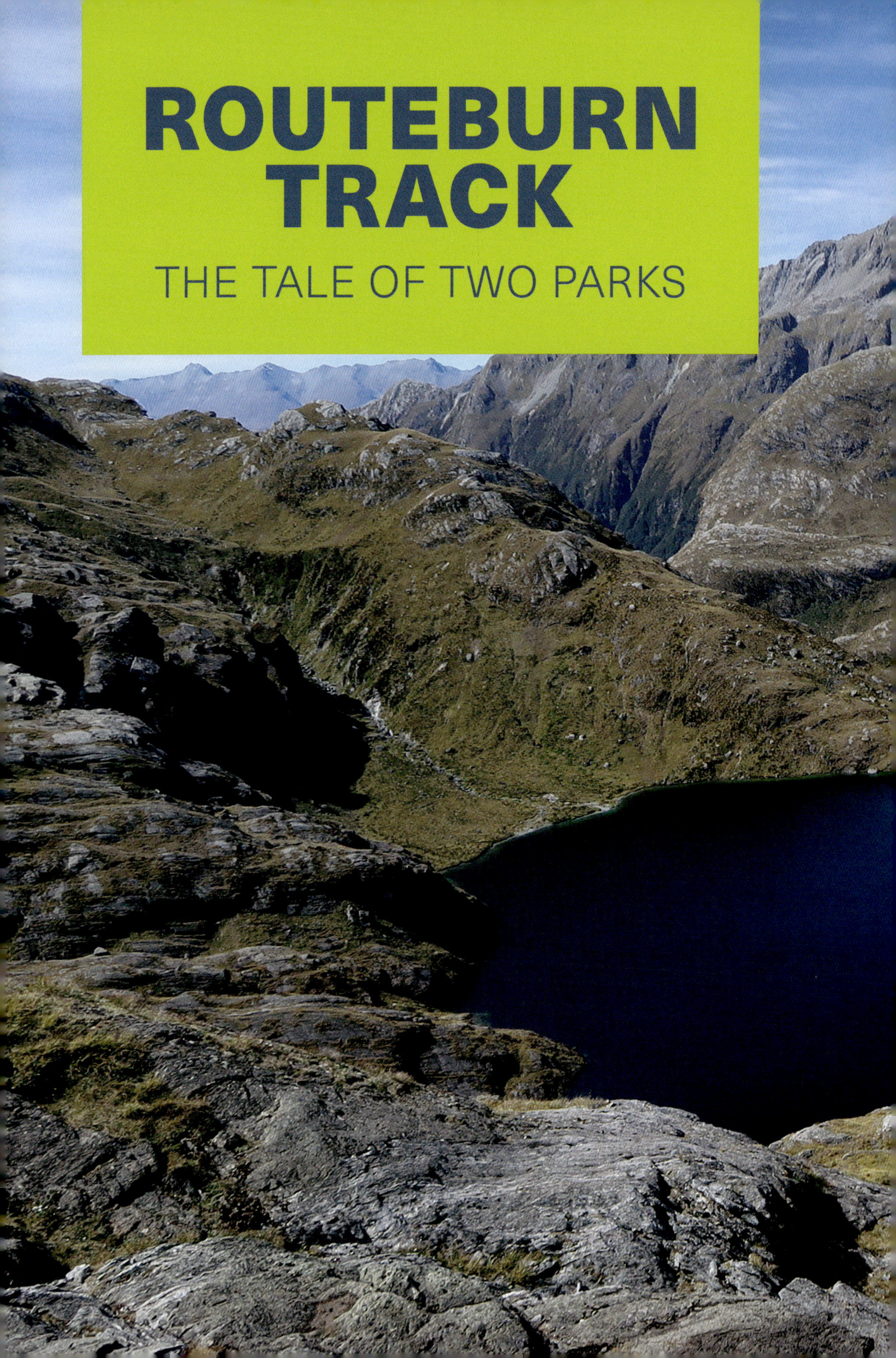

The view from Conical Hill looking over Lake Harris and the alpine section of the track.

ROUTEBURN TRACK

THE TALE OF TWO PARKS // 32 KM, 2–3 DAYS

— HIGHLIGHTS

- Do one of the world's most highly rated walks.
- Make an easily accessed alpine crossing.
- Relish the intimate and sublime beauty of Lake Mackenzie.
- Gain a unique perspective on the rugged Darran Mountains.
- Take your pick of alpine lakes to swim in.

BETWEEN THEM THE Fiordland and Mount Aspiring national parks cover more than 1600 square kilometres of New Zealand's South Island. This is mountainous country, with steep-walled valleys representing the slowly chiselled memories of once-huge glaciers that have long since melted to the sea. In summer the glacial remains – little more than pitted shadows of their former selves – can still be found on the shoulders of the highest mountains, while in the cold heart of winter much of the landscape becomes blanketed in snow.

The Routeburn Track forges a link between these two great tracts of land. Once voted by Lonely Planet as one of the world's best walks, it roughly follows an old trail used by Māori and then early European explorers, crossing between the Hollyford and Routeburn valleys as well as from one national park to the other.

Although it is not particularly long, the Routeburn Track passes through a varied and, at times, surprisingly intimate landscape, and it offers a unique perspective across Hollyford Valley to the Darran Mountains – a particularly jagged alpine area whose interior has been explored very little.

The approach to and crossing of Harris Saddle in the middle of the Routeburn Track carries with it a heady atmosphere, with cliff faces and

N
Somnus
Momus
HUMBOLDT
North Branch Route Burn >
MOUNT ASPIRING
NATIONAL PARK
< Hollyford River
Routeburn Gorge
Route Burn >
Routeburn Shelter
Conical Hill
Lake Harris
Routeburn Falls
Routeburn Flats
Harris Saddle
Harris Saddle Shelter
Emily Peak
DARRAN MOUNTAINS
MOUNTAINS
Lake Mackenzie
to Glenorchy
The Orchard
FIORDLAND
NATIONAL PARK
Earland Falls
AILSA MOUNTAINS
ford
Key Summit
Lake Howden
The Divide
Caples River >
94
Greenstone R. >
to Te Anau
0
5
10 km

mountains rising all around you, and perhaps a cool breeze blowing from the snowy summits of Fiordland's highest peaks, Mt Tūtoko and Mt Madeline, across the other side of the Hollyford Valley.

Here, and in some other locations along the track, you will need to watch where you place your feet, due to the precipitous nature of the country you are traversing, although it may be difficult to tear your eyes from the ever-changing views. In other places, you may find yourself stopping to marvel at yet another new scene, perhaps holding your breath in the realisation of how small you are in such a landscape of monumental grandeur.

TRACK DETAILS

LOCATION: Fiordland and Mount Aspiring national parks, Otago
TRACK TYPE: The Routeburn Track is a mountain traverse, crossing the Ailsa and Humboldt ranges. Initially starting in dense forest (assuming you begin from The Divide), the route climbs steadily up to the subalpine and alpine tops, crossing the exposed Harris Saddle at 1200 metres, before descending to forest again. Underfoot is a mixture of soil, gravel, boardwalk and, in places, uneven steps hewn from stone. Mostly the track is well maintained, but there are places where it is rough going and greater care will be needed. A walking pole is recommended.

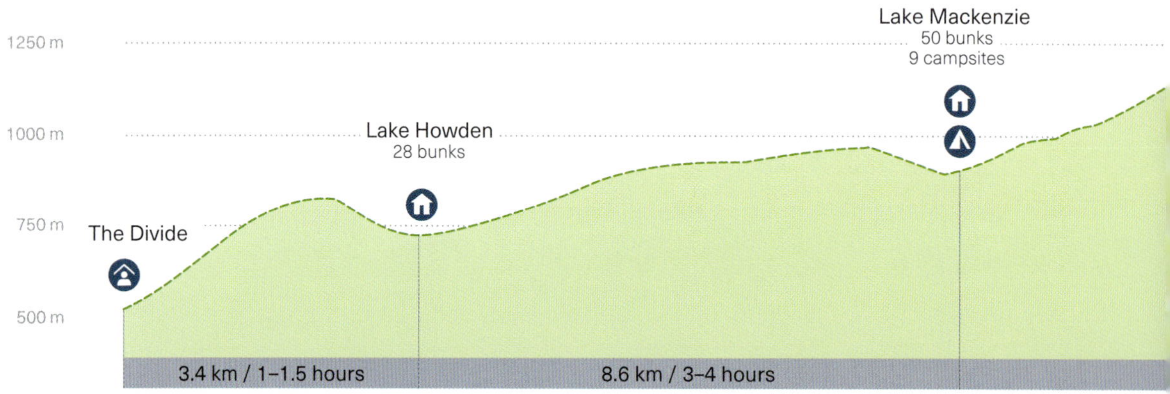

Climb from The Divide car park up through bush towards Key Summit.

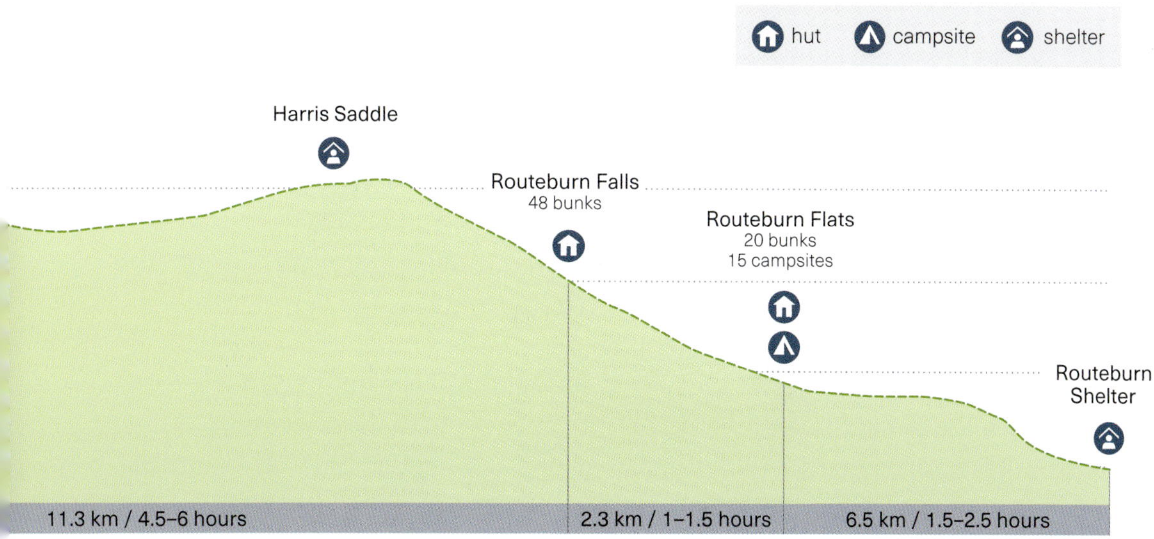

NOTE: This is a track to be completed *only* during the open season unless you have specific winter mountaineering equipment and specialist knowledge. In winter it can become covered in snow. Ill-equipped and inexperienced trampers have been killed here by avalanches and falls during the off season.

START POINT: The Divide or Routeburn Shelter
END POINT: Routeburn Shelter or The Divide
DISTANCE: 32 km
TIME: 2–3 days (although it can be done in a single day if you are in a hurry)
SEASON: 25 October – 3 May
GRADING: Moderate fitness required
DOC HUTS: Lake Howden (28 bunks), Mackenzie (50 bunks), Routeburn Falls (48 bunks), Routeburn Flats (20 bunks)
DOC CAMPSITES: Mackenzie (9 sites), Routeburn Flats (15 sites)

RECOMMENDED TRIP OPTION: Mackenzie Hut and Routeburn Falls Hut are set in awesomely scenic locations. Therefore the recommended trip is to start at The Divide, plan to spend a night at each of these huts (rather than Routeburn Flats and Lake Howden huts), and finish at Routeburn Shelter.

PLANNING

ACCESS: The Routeburn Track has two starting and finishing points and can be walked in either direction. One track end is at the Routeburn Shelter (near Glenorchy and 68 km from Queenstown). The other is at The Divide (on the Milford Highway, 85 km from Te Anau). It is at least 5 hours' driving between these two points, so you will need to arrange transport beforehand. There are plenty of commercial transport operators who can get you to and from the track or, if you prefer, take your vehicle from one end to the other.

If you are driving, please note that there have been a number of vehicle accidents involving tourists, especially on the Milford Highway. Also, be aware that the last portion of the drive from Glenorchy to the track is a narrow gravel road that should be driven with caution (sometimes there can be large buses coming in the other direction!).

The view from Key Summit.

ACCOMMODATION, FOOD AND EQUIPMENT: Queenstown and Te Anau have a full range (and price, from the reasonable to the ridiculous) of accommodation options. While Queenstown is unapologetically hedonistic – and busy – Te Anau can have a slower feel to it. This may determine which way round you prefer to walk the track.

Stock up on everything you will need before you leave Queenstown or Te Anau. There are no shops near either end of the track.

WEATHER: While this area gets much less rainfall than Milford Sound (see the Milford Track chapter), the higher, open section of the track is particularly exposed to what will sometimes be extreme mountain weather (strong winds, rain and snow). Check the forecast beforehand and, if you are unsure, ask one of the DOC officers stationed at the huts.

TRACK CONDITIONS: The middle portion of this track crosses an alpine environment and should be treated with the appropriate level of respect and caution. It is exposed to high winds, low visibility and the possibility of snow at any time of year. In poor conditions it may be advisable to turn around

Lake Mackenzie.

rather than risk the crossing – again, ask a DOC officer if you are unsure. Also, there are other parts of the track that can be treacherous when very wet. In times of heavy rainfall, small side streams could flood in minutes, and areas like Earland Falls should be avoided.

TRACK DESCRIPTION

The Divide to Lake Howden Hut: 1–2 hrs, 3 km

Access to The Divide is from State Highway 94 between Te Anau and Milford Sound. At 530 metres altitude, it is the lowest crossing of the 500 kilometre-long Southern Alps. From the Divide car park, a well-graded track climbs steadily through silver beech forest, allowing occasional views towards Mt Christina and the rest of the Darran Mountains, until reaching the top of the bushline, at a point just below an optional side track to the Key Summit.

It is worthwhile allowing for a few minutes' rest. Take in the sight of the

A track and boardwalk lead to the campsite at Lake Mackenzie.

mountainous terrain yet to be covered, now revealing itself before you. See if you can spot Harris Saddle in the distance, and marvel at the long sweep of the Hollyford Valley below your feet, stretching all the way to Martins Bay on the West Coast.

The side trip to Key Summit is a pretty cool uphill detour, and worth the effort especially when Lake Howden Hut is not far away on the main track. Indeed, the Divide car park to Key Summit trip is considered one of the best day walks in Fiordland, if not all of New Zealand. The high point at 919 metres offers a spectacular view. As you stand next to the small mountain tarn near the summit take a moment to imagine how, during the last ice age (which ended about 14,000 years ago), a glacier flowed down the Hollyford Valley before you and rose over Key Summit by some 500 metres, with huge corridors of ice branching off into both the Eglinton and Greenstone valleys.

Back on the main track, there is a 15 minute descent through the forest to Lake Howden Hut. From the hut another track traverses around the edge of Lake Howden to link up with the Greenstone and Caples tracks. These tracks can be combined with the Routeburn Track for a much longer circuit (described later).

Harris Saddle, with a view of the Darran Mountains behind.

Routeburn Falls Hut.

Lake Howden Hut to Mackenzie Hut: 3–4 hrs, 9 km

Leaving Lake Howden Hut, the track climbs steadily through more beech forest, and past the impressive Earland Falls (174 m high), where there is a detour if the falls are in flood. Further on, you will come to an open, grassy area with a number of ribbonwood trees, which is known as the Orchard. Note that parts of this section of track may be tricky underfoot as it continues through more forest, before finally descending to Mackenzie Hut and the picturesque Lake Mackenzie.

Emily Peak rises before you. You will traverse around this mountain, then descend into the Routeburn Valley on its other side. While the water in the lake will likely be cool, even in summer, it is still worth a refreshing dip on a warm afternoon. The Mackenzie Campsite, situated a few more minutes' walk past the hut, is a recommended place to stay if you are considering bringing a tent.

Mackenzie Hut to Routeburn Falls Hut: 4–6 hrs, 11 km

As you leave Mackenzie Hut, before you rises the alpine portion of the track. Be aware that this is exposed to the elements, with sudden storms rolling in from the Tasman Sea only a few kilometres to the west. Care is needed, especially in poor weather and low visibility.

But, for the first part at least, you needn't worry. Immediately past Mackenzie Hut is a section of track with a photogenic and aptly described 'goblin forest' of stunted beech. After you leave the shelter of the forest the track climbs up wide grass shelves above the lake, leading to the exposed Hollyford Face.

Staying above the bush now, you traverse the Hollyford Face, continuing a gradual ascent through open tussock land, eventually reaching the shelter and a well-earned rest at Harris Saddle (1255 m).

If you have enough energy and the weather is settled, a popular side trip from the saddle is to scramble up to the summit of nearby Conical Hill (1500 m), which offers 360-degree views of the area, including out along the Hollyford Valley to Martins Bay. Be aware, this steep track can have snow and ice on it even during the open season.

After leaving the saddle, you begin a gradual descent towards the Routeburn Valley, at first following the track around a cliff perched over another appealing lake, Lake Harris. The track winds between rocky outcrops, offering great views to the east, and eventually down to the lake and an area of wetlands and more tussock flats. The constant tumble of water running from the outlet of Lake Harris accompanies you as you approach the top edge of the bushline again, nearing the impressive Routeburn Falls, and finally the sheltered and pristine setting of Routeburn Falls Hut.

Routeburn Falls Hut to Routeburn Flats Hut: 1–1.5 hrs, 2 km

Leaving the hut, the track drops steadily through more beech forest, providing occasional views of the Humboldt Mountains nearby. Emily Creek marks halfway on the descent towards Flats Hut. There is a small risk of loose rock (especially during and just after rainfall) at Phoenix Bluff, where the track crosses the old scar of a massive slip from 1994; the area is highlighted with signposts, and it pays not to dawdle here.

Offering occasional views through the trees, the track descends to grassy flats that spread into the north branch of the Routeburn River. The impressive Mt Somnus (2293 m) and Mt Momus (2148 m) – popular climbing objectives – rise above them.

This area of the track is where you might be more likely to see a rare mohua (yellowhead) and even hear the cry of a kākā, before levelling out close to the turn-off to Routeburn Flats Hut. The hut is set near the large area of open grass flats that could be seen earlier. If you still have the energy, an optional side trail leads across the flats to the north branch of the Routeburn.

Routeburn Flats Hut to Routeburn Shelter: 1.5–3 hrs, 7 km

The track continues along the banks of the Routeburn River towards a gradual narrowing of the land, eventually leading into the Routeburn Gorge (which would have been visible from up high at the balcony outside Routeburn Falls Hut).

Never far from the roar of running water, you trek beneath red and silver beech, listening for the calls of bellbirds and other songbirds. The South Island robins found through this portion of forest can be quite cheeky, sometimes even standing in the middle of the track and forcing you to detour around them. Keep an eye out for some impressive gorges carved through rock in the main river, as well as side streams, before the valley opens again and you eventually reach Routeburn Shelter.

POINTS OF INTEREST

Greenstone trail

The first humans in the Routeburn area were likely to have been Māori around AD 1500, travelling in search of the valuable and versatile New Zealand pounamu. The Routeburn did not yield large quantities of the greenstone, but it was a pathway between the Arahura River on the West Coast and the Dart Valley, which were two main sources.

Descending to the
Routeburn Valley.

Looking across the Routeburn Flats to the north branch of the Routeburn Valley.

European exploration

The first Europeans here were George Gunn and David McKellar in 1861, mapping the area as they searched for suitable grazing land for stock. When gold was discovered nearby, the government looked at establishing a port on the West Coast to transport the precious metal overseas. A track up the Routeburn Valley and over Harris Saddle to the Hollyford Valley was started but then abandoned in 1870. However, the Routeburn route did remain an important link between the families choosing to settle in the Hollyford Valley and the growing commercial centre of Wakatipu.

The birth of local tourism

Around the 1880s, the first Pākehā sightseers from Queenstown began to explore the Routeburn Valley. Work on the track restarted after the government set up the Department of Tourism in the early 1900s. The search for a direct route from Harris Saddle to Lake Howden in 1912 led to the discovery of Lake Mackenzie. But with construction of the track halted during World War I, the newer portion was not completed till the 1930s.

Bringing the birds back

The Routeburn area has been a focal point for a number of conservation projects involving DOC and various other private and commercial partners, all keen to restore native bird populations. Being a narrow valley with established forest and surrounded by high peaks, the Routeburn is recognised as a suitable mainland site for bird protection. Species such as the rock wren, kākā and mohua (yellowhead) used to thrive in the headwaters of Lake Wakatipu, but stoats have decimated their numbers. The problem is most acute in high beech tree masting years: the extra seeds spur an explosion in mouse numbers, and this glut of prey in turn boosts stoat numbers; the predators often turn their attention from mice to local birds, which can be easier to hunt.

Recent trapping programmes by DOC and groups including the Routeburn Dart Wildlife Trust, and a reintroduction of focused bird species such as the mohua, have helped to begin the re-establishment of some of our rare and endangered wildlife.

Blue duck reintroduction

The native whio (or blue duck), is one of only a handful of torrent duck species in the world. Endemic to New Zealand, it inhabits clean, fast-flowing streams in the forested upper catchments of our rivers. But it is highly vulnerable to habitat disturbance and to predators (females on the nest are at great risk from stoats), and today there are fewer than 3000 birds left. Recently, small numbers of whio have been translocated into the Routeburn catchment to help re-establish the population here. During your walk along the flats section of the track, you may be lucky enough to see some in the river.

OFF THE TRACK

After completing the Routeburn Track, you could spend your time celebrating with a multitude of other partygoers in Queenstown or, at a gentler pace, in Te Anau. Or, you could make the most of where you are, and get out and about to see what some of the other nearby tracks are like.

Greenstone/Caples tracks

As mentioned earlier, the Caples and Greenstone tracks can be linked with the Routeburn Track, walked as a one-way track (taking around 4 days in total) starting or finishing either at The Divide or the Greenstone Shelter. The Greenstone Valley is wide and open, with tussock flats and beech forest. In comparison, the Caples Valley is narrower, and filled with forest interspersed with grassy clearings. Both valleys are linked by a subalpine pass, the McKellar Saddle. The route is a moderately demanding tramp (much more so than the Routeburn on its own), with some days averaging 6–7 hours of steady walking.

Hollyford Track

For those who like to venture a little further off the beaten track, but still have a good standard of track and huts to stay in, the Hollyford Track is an enjoyable tramping adventure. Beginning at the end of the long gravel Hollyford Valley Road, and set beneath the rock walls of the Darran Mountains, the track follows the Hollyford River on its winding journey to the ocean at Martins Bay. There aren't any exposed alpine sections on the track, so it is very rarely cut off by snow or other adverse conditions, and therefore can usually be tramped in any season.

Cascade Saddle route

This is a more demanding track if you are looking to build up to another challenge. Cascade Saddle is an alpine pass between the West Matukituki and Dart valleys, and the saddle route, which links the Matukituki with the Rees-Dart Track, is a popular summer trip for suitably experienced trampers. Taking 1–2 days to complete, the route does not cross the actual Cascade Saddle – which is impassable from the Matukituki – but rather passes within a short distance of it on the Dart side. Being an alpine pass, this route crosses terrain that may require basic mountaineering skills. If you are interested, contact DOC for more information and an up-to-date report on conditions on the pass.

Earland Falls.

Mackinnon Pass, the highest point, is about halfway along the track.

MILFORD TRACK

THE FINEST WALK IN THE WORLD

MILFORD TRACK

THE FINEST WALK IN THE WORLD // 53 KM, 4 DAYS

— HIGHLIGHTS

- » Enjoy an hour-long boat ride across Lake Te Anau.
- » Take in the views at Mackinnon Pass and Milford Sound.
- » Walk up to the base of New Zealand's tallest waterfall.
- » Consider the human history of the area.
- » Appreciate the scale of this remote landscape.

AROUND A HUNDRED years ago, poet Blanche Baughan declared New Zealand's remote Milford Track to be 'the finest walk in the world'. While these days the Milford gets decent local competition from the nearby Kepler and Routeburn, the track remains the pinnacle for providing stunning and surprisingly intimate alpine views. On the Mackinnon Pass especially, the peaks are so close that you feel you can reach out and touch them.

This is a land of long waterfalls and sheer rock walls, glaciers perched high on the rumps of mountains, and avalanche paths demonstrating just how severe nature can be.

Arguably still New Zealand's most famous walk, the 53 kilometre journey begins at the head of Lake Te Anau, from where it leads up the Clinton Valley, over Mackinnon Pass and down the Arthur Valley to finish at Milford Sound. The track cuts through the heart of Fiordland, one of the world's great wilderness regions. Fiordland has been a national park since 1952 and a World Heritage area since 1986. There are 14 main fiords here, ranging from Preservation Inlet in the south to Milford Sound in the north. According to southern Māori traditions, all of them are the creations of Tū Te Rakiwhānoa, an atua (god) who shaped the local landscape with his magical adze.

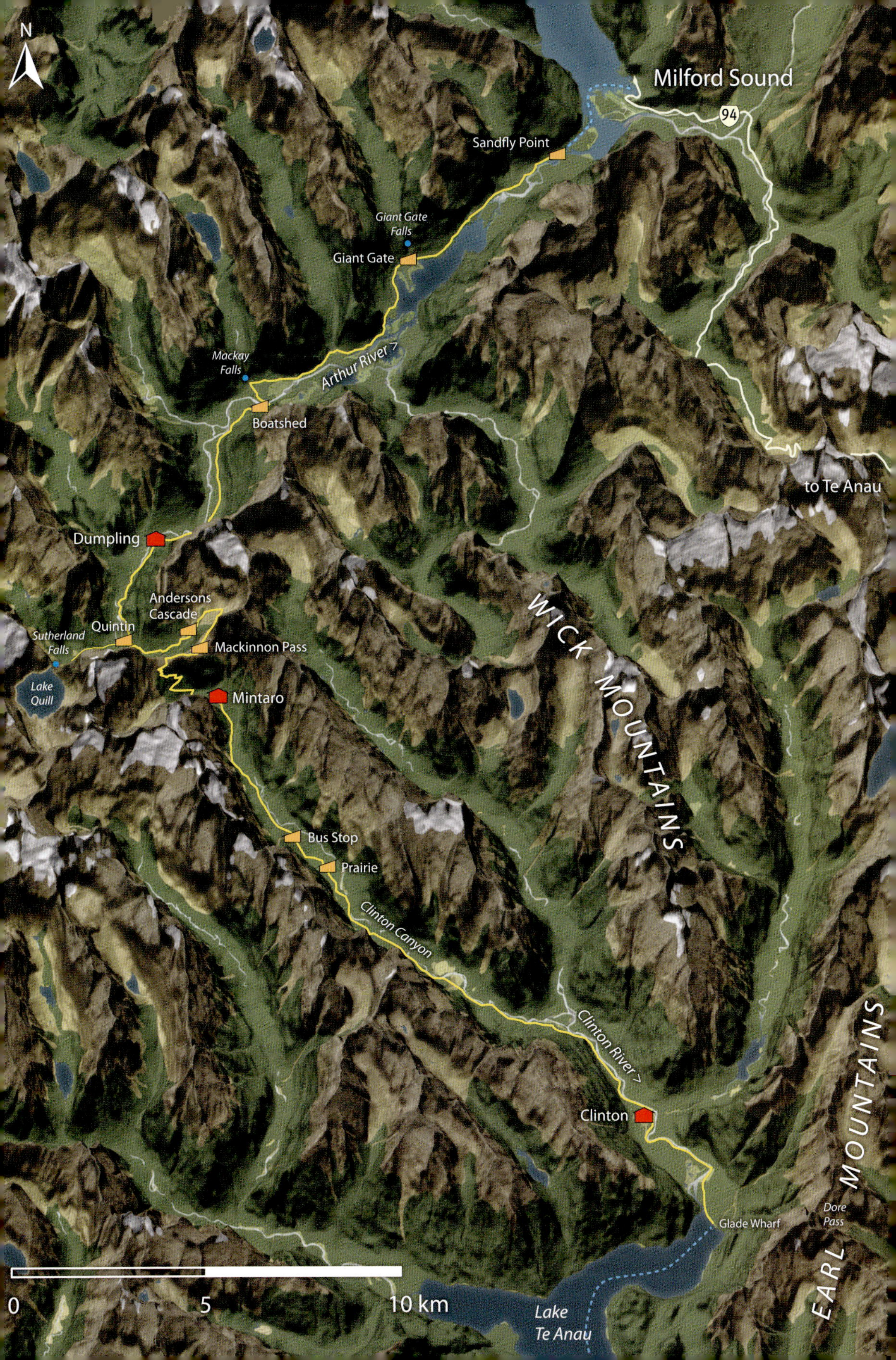

N
Milford Sound
94
Sandfly Point
Giant Gate Falls
Giant Gate
Mackay Falls
Arthur River >
Boatshed
to Te Anau
Dumpling
Andersons Cascade
Quintin
Sutherland Falls
Mackinnon Pass
Lake Quill
Mintaro
WICK MOUNTAINS
Bus Stop
Prairie
Clinton Canyon
Clinton River >
Clinton
EARL MOUNTAINS
Glade Wharf
Dore Pass
0
5
10 km
Lake Te Anau

Milford Sound is the most accessible of the fiords, being the only one reached by road. It was incorrectly named as a sound, but by the time the mistake was realised, the name was so well known that it was decided not to change it. (A fiord is created by glacial flow, whereas a sound is eroded by a river.)

With its stunning view of Mitre Peak, Milford Sound at the end of the track is considered the best-known and most visited of New Zealand's scenic attractions. Yet although it receives around 400,000 visitors annually, Milford Sound has a permanent population of only 60–200 (depending on the time of year), made up of staff from the cruise boats and the Milford Track and hotel, and the local fisher folk who harvest crayfish off the coast. With the exception of Milford Sound Lodge (a motor camp/backpackers) and Mitre Peak Lodge, which is the last hut for the track and the overnight cruise boats, there is no accommodation at Milford Sound. The closest accommodation is in Te Anau, 2 hours' drive away.

The overwhelming majority of visitors to Milford Sound come and leave in a single day. They trundle in by bus, hoping to get a photo of Mitre Peak and perhaps take a boat ride on the sound, before returning inland. This seems scant time to appreciate such a stunning environment. So it is indeed a special opportunity, if not a privilege, to walk the Milford Track and get to appreciate this environment over several days.

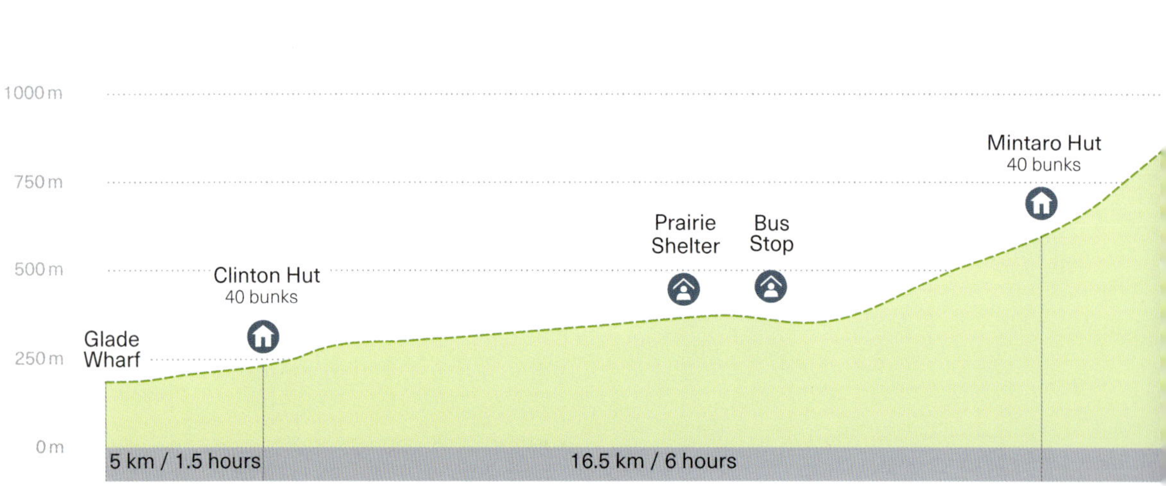

Board a boat at Te Anau Downs to get to the start of the track.

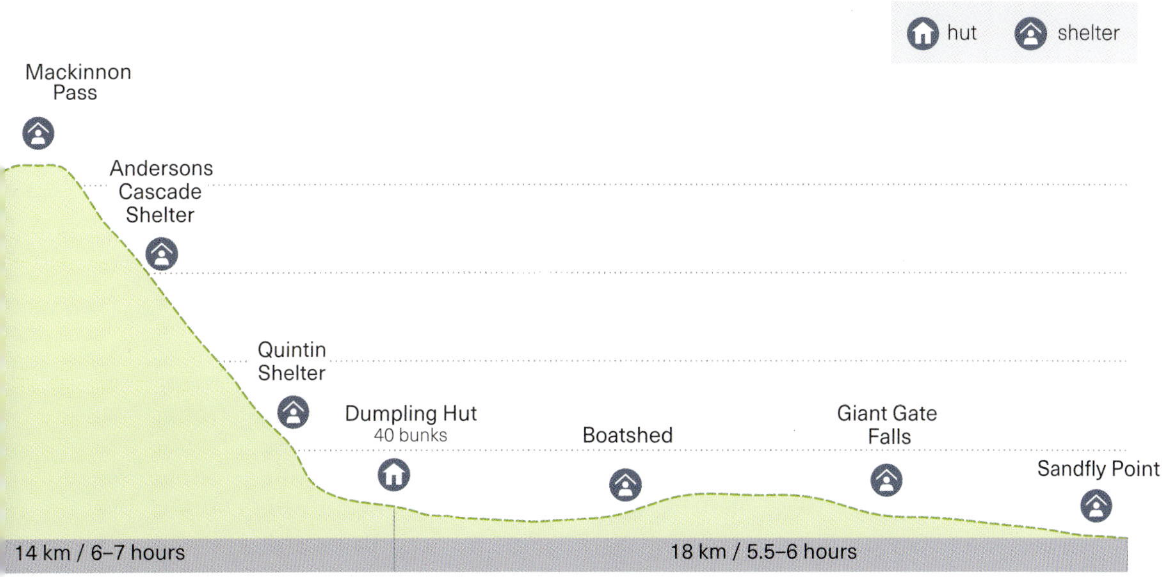

TRACK DETAILS

LOCATION: Fiordland National Park, Fiordland
TRACK TYPE: This is a through track, starting at Glade Wharf at the head of Lake Te Anau (after an hour-long boat ride from Te Anau Downs), and finishing at Sandfly Point in Milford Sound. Taking 4 days to complete, it is walked in only one direction. The only accommodation is at pre-booked huts (there is no camping along the track).
NOTE: Much of the Milford Track may be threatened by avalanches at certain times of the year. It is to be completed only during the open season unless you have winter mountaineering equipment and knowledge. Sometimes, helicopters are required to transfer walkers over avalanche-prone sections in the early season (or very occasionally after a snowstorm).

START POINT: Te Anau Downs
END POINT: Milford Sound
DISTANCE: 53 km
TIME: 4 days
SEASON: 24 October – 3 May
GRADING: There is a decent climb up to Mackinnon Pass, and some of the terrain through this section can be a little tricky underfoot, especially during the descent into the Arthur Valley. Otherwise, the track is very straightforward and of a gentle gradient. Moderate fitness is required.
DOC HUTS: Clinton (40 bunks), Mintaro (40 bunks), Dumpling (40 bunks)

RECOMMENDED TRIP OPTION: The track and huts are likely to be fully booked ahead and behind you, so you will need to take the full 4 days. Luckily this is a great way to enjoy the scenery.

PLANNING

ACCESS: Travel to and from the Milford Track requires road transport and boat access at both ends. Te Anau is a good place to base yourself and leave

Crossing the Clinton River.

your vehicle, instead using one of the local operators (boat and vehicle) to get you to Te Anau Downs and back from Milford Sound. It's around half an hour by road to Te Anau Downs and 2 hours' drive back from the sound. The boat ride in to the track takes just over an hour, and there is another 15 minute ride at the end, from Sandfly Point to Milford Sound. You will need to book all of these before starting the track.

There is alternative access to the start of the track, via a route over Dore Pass from the Eglinton Valley, but it is difficult going, and for experienced trampers only.

ACCOMMODATION, FOOD AND EQUIPMENT: Te Anau has a full range of accommodation and food options along with a well-stocked outdoors store. Be sure to get everything you need (including insect repellent) before leaving Te Anau as there are no shops at either end of the track.

WEATHER: Fiordland is renowned for its rainfall as well as snowfall in winter. Milford Sound, with 6–7 metres of rain a year, is probably the wettest inhabited place in New Zealand and one of the wettest in the world. With this in mind it is advisable to take a particularly sturdy raincoat and be prepared for rain (which at least keeps the sandflies away).

TRACK CONDITIONS: The middle portion of this track crosses Mackinnon Pass, which is an alpine environment and should be treated with appropriate

Clinton Hut.

respect and caution. The top part of the pass is across open country, and is exposed to high winds, low visibility and the possibility of snow at any time of year. In poor conditions it may be advisable to turn around rather than risk the crossing. Other parts of the track may flood during or after heavy rainfall. Check conditions with DOC beforehand.

TRACK DESCRIPTION

Glade Wharf to Clinton Hut: 1–1.5 hrs, 5 km

Really, the first part of the journey begins at Te Anau Downs when you board the boat that will take you to the start of the track. Have your camera ready during the boat ride, as the Earl Mountains to your right, the Franklin Mountains to your left and the Wick Mountains straight ahead all seem to draw in around you. At its northernmost reach, the lake is surprisingly narrow with plenty to hold your attention during the hour-long journey. Once you're unloaded at Glade Wharf, the start of the track is a very gentle walk through beech forest and then along the banks of the Clinton River to get to the clearing surrounding Clinton Hut. There are some great swimming holes close to the hut and also a short boardwalk around a nearby wetland area.

Clinton Hut to Mintaro Hut: 6 hrs, 16 km

Cross a swing bridge over the Clinton River soon after leaving the hut. The track continues up the Clinton Valley, usually not far from the Clinton River with its deep, clear pools and rock-filled rapids. Occasionally the forest parts enough to show how steeply the mountains rise on either side.

Note that you are passing beneath a number of avalanche paths, but DOC has placed signs out highlighting the 'No Stopping' zones. In heavy rain, a portion of this part of the track can become submerged. Wading may be necessary! On the plus side, there should be lots of spectacular waterfalls pouring from the cliffs either side of you.

As you gain more altitude, there is a change in vegetation. Beech forest gives way to wild fuchsia in places. The mountains feel very close now on both sides and, with more open country on the valley floor, you are better able to appreciate the view of the pass you will need to climb at the head of the valley. Mintaro Hut is nestled into an area of forest just before the angle of the track steepens considerably for the ascent to Mackinnon Pass.

Mintaro Hut to Dumpling Hut: 6–7 hrs, 14 km

This is a particularly spectacular day! Leaving Mintaro Hut, the track zigzags through forest and then alpine grasses as you gain elevation. You are in a cirque of mountains now, with riflemen and rock wrens to keep you company during the slog to Mackinnon Pass (a total of around 550 m in height gain from Mintaro Hut).

There is a memorial at the pass for explorer Quintin McKinnon, but more likely you will be entranced by the exceptional views back down the Clinton Valley and into the Arthur Valley, which lies ahead of you. The pass shelter (the highest point of the track at 1154 metres) is a great place to stop for lunch, before the steep and rocky descent towards the valley floor, down a bunch of wooden stairs, passing Andersons Cascade Shelter and several waterfalls along the Roaring Burn River before arriving at Quintin Shelter. Be sure to take the side trip to Sutherland Falls, another definite highlight (the falls drop 580 metres in three stages from Lake Quill), before carrying on along the last section of track to Dumpling Hut.

Climbing up to Mackinnon Pass.

Dumpling Hut to Sandfly Point: 5–6 hrs, 18 km

The last day is a gentle decline along the banks of the Arthur River. Mostly you will be sheltered by beech forest, but sometimes you will pass through open country allowing views of more mountains rising around you. There is a short side trip to Mackay Falls before carrying on to the aptly named Sandfly Point, from which a short boat ride takes you to the end of your journey at Milford Sound.

POINTS OF INTEREST

Local early explorer Donald Sutherland was evidently a talented man. In 1877 he sailed a small boat from Thompson Sound to Milford Sound, completing the 96 kilometre journey in this remote south-western corner of the South Island in an impressive 10 hours.

Clearly, Scottish-born Sutherland liked what he found. The sheer rock walls dropping over 1500 metres down into the narrow waters of Milford Sound would have been a mesmerising sight. And with no land access back then, Sutherland must have felt as though he had arrived at the ends of the earth.

Returning a few weeks later with more supplies, Sutherland began building a shelter at Freshwater Basin, where the current Milford Wharf stands. Over the course of the following months he built a cottage, and then two more huts, naming his new home the 'City of Milford'.

The land where Sutherland built his lodgings offered a clear view of the magnificent Mitre Peak, and in 1883 he finally decided to climb it. Along with Samuel Moreton, an artist visiting from Invercargill, Sutherland tried to scramble up the steep-sided peak from the head of Sinbad Gully. The pair reached a narrow ridge line some distance west of the summit, and had to turn back. The mountain was finally climbed in 1911 by J R Dennistoun, after Sutherland had advised him to attempt it from the eastern side.

Apart from occasional visits to Dunedin, Donald Sutherland lived a hermit-like existence in Milford Sound during the early to mid-1880s, receiving only the occasional visitor via the steamer service. He went prospecting for diamonds in Sinbad Gully with the historian James Cowan,

The Mackinnon Pass Shelter.

and discovered Sutherland Falls – although, perhaps through excitement, he greatly overestimated its height at 1500 metres. Sutherland searched unsuccessfully for gold, but then slowly began to realise that there was a growing demand from visitors. So did the government, which paid him to cut a track to the falls. During the summer of 1888–89, around 40 people visited the falls. Tourism had landed at Milford Sound.

Sutherland eventually married Elizabeth Samuels, a widow. Samuels brought not only vision to the venture, but also cash: she arranged to buy a site on which the couple built an accommodation house, the Chalet, to cater for the now burgeoning summer tourist trade. This was around the same time as the opening of the Milford Track. Although it is likely Māori knew of the route long beforehand, surveyor Quinton McKinnon and companion Ernest Mitchell 'discovered' what has now become an incredibly popular track – a pass from the Clinton Valley at the head of Lake Te Anau which led over the Arthur Range and into Milford Sound. Author Rudyard Kipling was among the visitors in 1891, travelling to Milford Sound at the age of 24. He later described the sound as the 'eighth wonder of the world', an adulation that helped the area grow into an icon of New Zealand tourism.

Descending into the Arthur Valley.

The McKinnon memorial at Mackinnon Pass.

Development of a legacy

The Milford area remained accessible only by boat for many decades; nevertheless, its reputation continued to grow. The New Zealand government was keen to take advantage of this, encouraging the search for land-based access from Otago or Southland. From Lake Te Anau, Quintin McKinnon sought an overland tourist route into Milford Sound, and in 1888 discovered what is now named Mackinnon Pass; the route he pioneered is now, essentially, the Milford Track. McKinnon began guiding tours himself – he was the first to guide walkers from Lake Te Anau to Milford Sound – and the operation quickly expanded after a marketing campaign. The government controlled the track and guided tours from 1901 until 1990, when it was sold to a private enterprise.

Not surprisingly, given its history, the Milford has become the most controlled of our Great Walks. While only commercially guided groups were allowed on the track for a number of decades, it took a stand by the Otago Tramping Club (OTC) to open it up to non-paying walkers. In 1965, 46 members of the OTC organised a 'freedom walk' along the track in protest. And the protest worked: a year later plans were in place for additional huts and facilities for independent walkers.

Land access to Milford Sound

Explorers William Grave and Arthur Talbot took up the challenge of finding land access to Milford Sound, spending many summers exploring the nearby Darran Mountains and looking for a route over the high passes. In January 1910 they discovered and established Talbot's Ladder, an exposed and dangerous rocky spur that led on to Grave-Talbot Pass and which later became a mail trail into the sound.

At the time it was still hoped that a tourist path could be constructed using this route. But sanity prevailed. After lobbying by a Mr J Cockburn of the Southland Progress League, the decision was made to start on a tunnel. In 1935, five men with shovels and wheelbarrows began digging what would, eventually, become the 1240-metre-long Homer tunnel from the Hollyford side into the Cleddau Valley, and Milford Sound beyond.

Although the number of tunnel workers increased, this was still difficult and dangerous country to work in. Heavy rainfall, snowfall, and the risk of avalanches took their toll. In July 1936 a tunneller was killed and others injured when an avalanche hit the entrance. The following year another two were killed. Then World War II halted work, followed by another huge avalanche in 1945 that destroyed much of the access. Finally, in the summer of 1954, the first private car drove through the Homer tunnel, which now caters to over 250,000 vehicles each year. And one of the world's best avalanche monitoring systems was installed to keep the road as safe as possible.

OFF THE TRACK

Explore Milford Sound

After walking the Milford Track, you will have come to realise just how rugged and mostly inaccessible this landscape is. With that in mind, there are few options in the area that allow for more exploration. To see more of Milford Sound, take either a scenic boat trip or, for something more active, a kayak trip in the sound. Several companies run Milford Sound kayaking tours, with a wide range catering to your skill level, your sense of adventure and the amount of time you can spare. Whether you're an experienced paddler or a beginner who has never sat in a kayak before, you are sure to find a tour to suit.

Walk up Tūtoko Valley

Not far from Milford Sound there is an interesting up-and-back track starting near the Tūtoko River. This is a challenging tramping route, quite a step up from the well-formed Milford Track, and should be attempted only in settled weather.

Look for a small car park at the signposted Tutuko River bridge. From here it is about a 2 hour hike along a marked but rough track through dense forest on the true right of the river. Eventually you will come to a clearing in the valley beyond the bushline, where there is a spectacular view of the steep-walled mountains on either side of you, including the highest local peak, Mt Tutuko (2745 m).

Scramble up to Gertrude Saddle

This has become quite a popular tourist trip, and for good reason. Starting near Homer Hut (close to Homer Tunnel), follow the track markers up to an awesome view down towards Milford Sound.

Climb Mitre Peak

Although often photographed, Mitre Peak is climbed relatively rarely, and for good reason. What appears quite close is actually a 3-kilometre-long east ridge rising steadily and steeply to the summit at 1683 metres. The summit of Mitre Peak is an exposed climb, with the very real risk of falling all the way to the sound far below. Most people who attempt it camp at a saddle between the Footstool and Mitre Peak. (Note that there is no reliable water source here, so you will have to carry enough for your whole trip.)

While it is exciting and spectacular, if not too technically challenging in the scramble up through the bush to the open tops, the rocky pyramid of Mitre Peak is for experienced climbers only. Most climbers tend to use a rope for the final, very exposed section.

You can get the same views over the sound below, and avoid the riskiest climbing, by just scrambling up to an obvious notch in the ridge and returning from there. If, however, you are determined to step foot on the very top, there are guiding companies that can lead you there.

Arthur River – heading towards Milford Sound.

Climbing above Lake Te Anau.

KEPLER TRACK

THE EDGE OF NOTHING

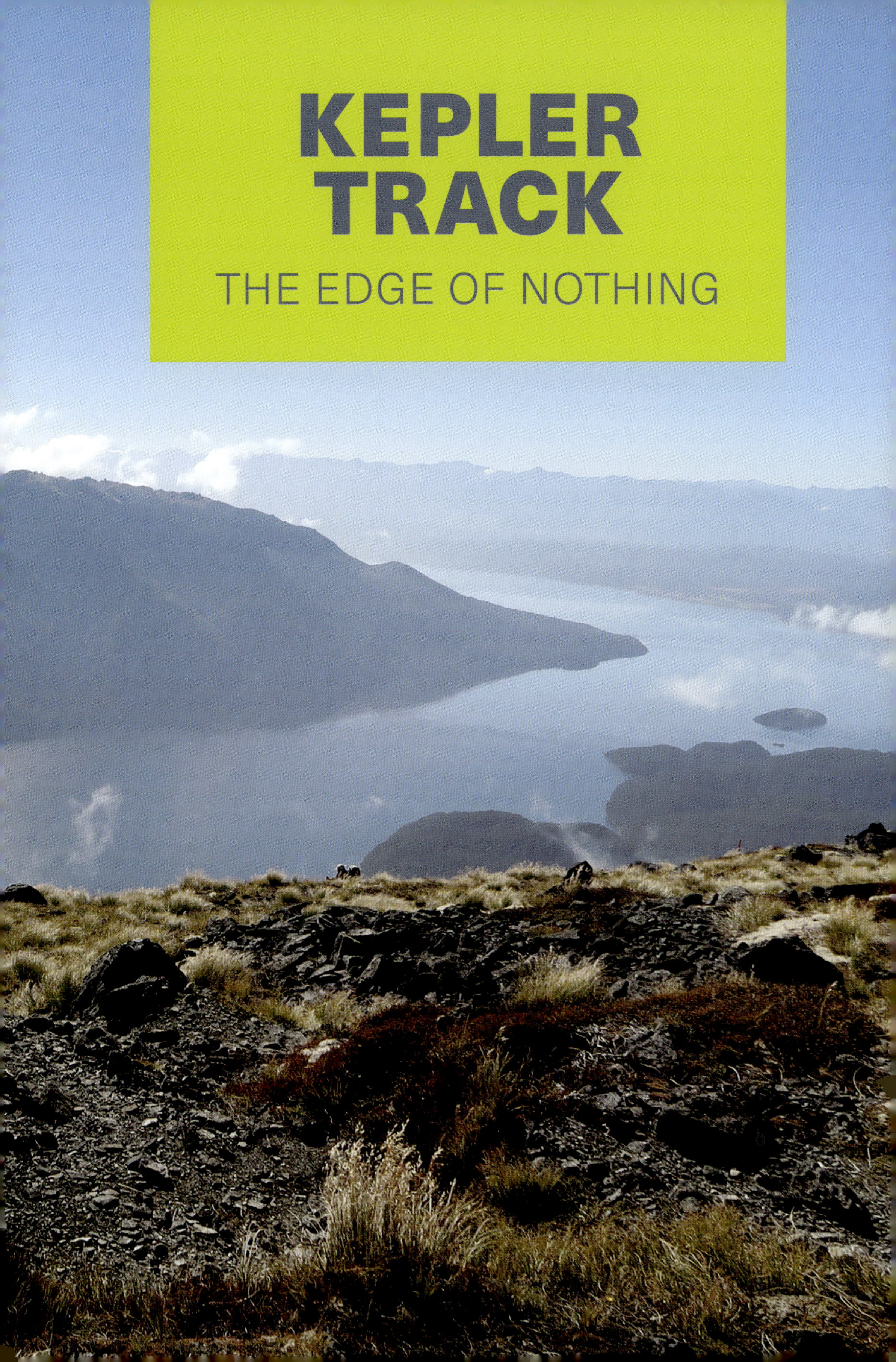

KEPLER TRACK

THE EDGE OF NOTHING // 64 KM, 2–4 DAYS

— HIGHLIGHTS

- Make a spectacular and sustained alpine crossing.
- Hear the cries of kea and watch them in their natural environment.
- See a unique perspective on Fiordland's rugged interior.
- Travel easily through low-lying forest filled with birdsong.
- Take side trips that include a mountain summit and an alpine cave.

THE SOUTH-WESTERN CORNER of Aotearoa New Zealand is bush-choked and fiord-gouged. Even today, few roads or tracks pierce this austere, mountainous country. At 12,500 square kilometres, Fiordland is our country's largest national park.

Smoothed surfaces of dark glacial lakes reflect a land that's challenging to explore, where swift rivers cut between steep-walled canyons, and thickset forests remain untroubled by the few who pass through them. From the forest floor, marbled light flickers between latticed branches, the canopy gaps allowing only brief glimpses of the high mountains. For those who travel here, gathering anything other than a peripheral – but still overwhelming – sense of the landscape requires effort.

The palm-like Lake Te Anau, on the eastern edge of the national park, is Australasia's largest internal body of water (by volume). Its many tapered fingers, or fiords, slice into the interior of Fiordland, cutting narrow pathways through the forests and between the mountain ranges.

This land was described by early European explorers in the 1700s as 'nothing . . . to be seen but barren mountains with huge craggy precipices frightful to behold', and little has changed in the time since. According to the local Ngāti Māmoe people, they used to take refuge from their

N
0
5
10 km
MURCHISON MOUNTAINS
South Fiord
Lake Te Anau
Hanging Valley
Luxmore
Mt Luxmore
cave
Forest Burn
urn
Iris Burn
Jackson Peaks
Brod Bay
Te Anau
Control Gates
Kepler Track Car Park
Rocky Point
Iris Burn
Moturau
Shallow Bay
Rainbow Reach
Waiau River
95
Lake Manapōuri
to Manapōuri

enemies in the high country here, building a maze of secret trails in dense woodlands between the great lakes of Te Anau and Manapōuri.

These days, the town of Te Anau, nestled near the southernmost edge of Lake Te Anau, is the starting point for the Kepler Track. The route takes you along forested shorelines and on to a high alpine traverse which offers views about as spectacular as any in New Zealand. Unlike the shorter alpine passes on the other Great Walks mentioned in this book, on the mountain section of the Kepler you are high above the shelter of the forest for most of the day. You will follow the spine of a ridge as it winds past the summit of Mt Luxmore (1472 m), with the South Fiord of Lake Te Anau beneath your feet on one side and the craggy Jackson Peaks and Kepler Mountains rising above you on the other. Follow this narrow pathway with the knowledge that you, too, are within reach of those 'huge craggy precipices', walking in a terrain that truly seems to be on the edge of nothing.

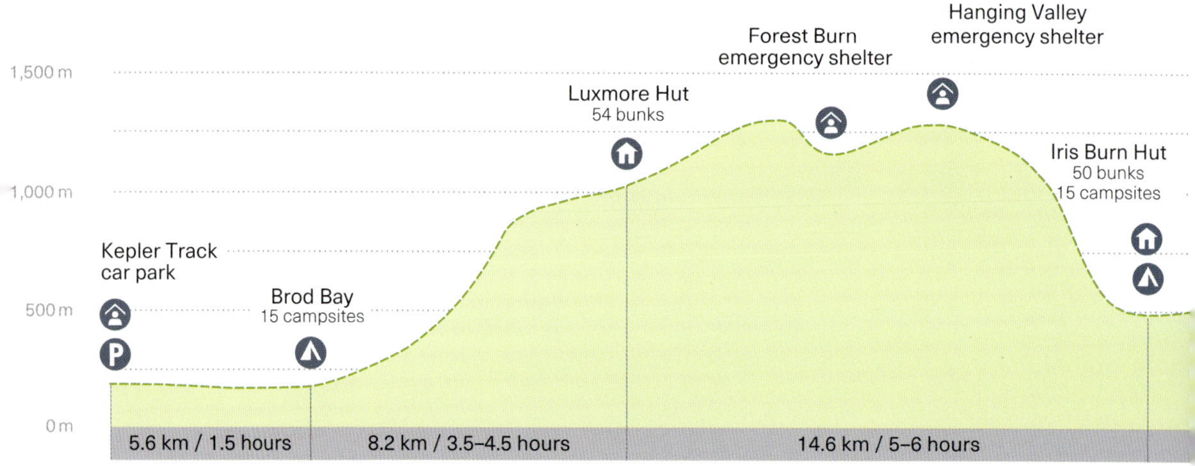

The track leading up to Luxmore Hut.

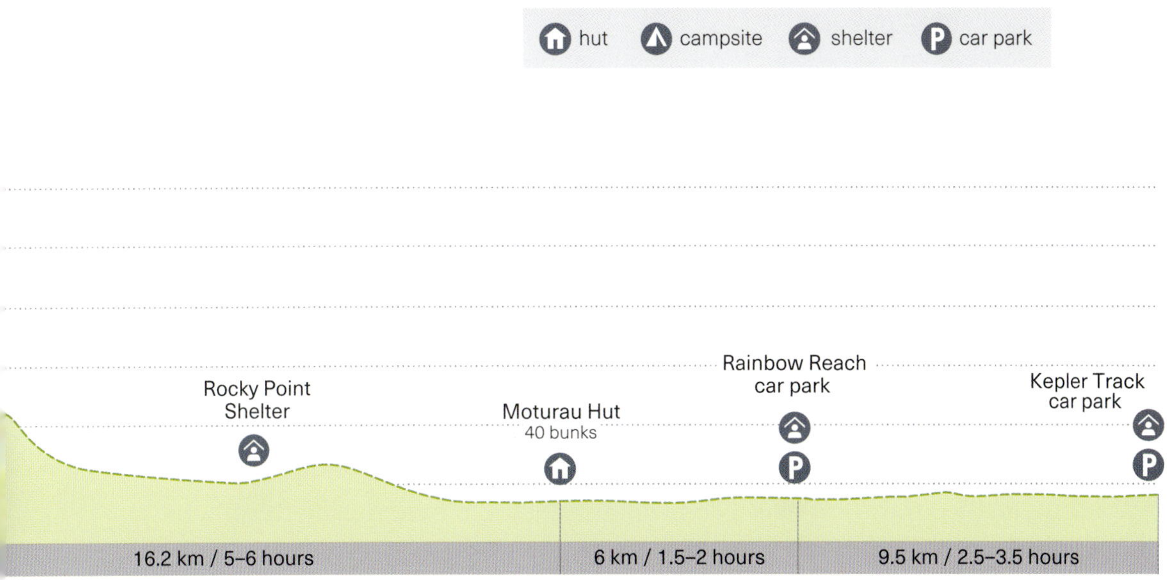

Luxmore Hut.

TRACK DETAILS

LOCATION: Fiordland National Park, Fiordland

TRACK TYPE: This is a circular mountain traverse, climbing up to and crossing a portion of the Jackson Peaks and Kepler Mountains between Lake Te Anau and Lake Manapōuri. Beginning in beech and podocarp forest, the route skirts the edge of Lake Te Anau before ascending steadily to the subalpine zone and then the alpine tops, passing just beneath Mt Luxmore and nearby open country, before eventually descending to forest again. It is a mixture of soil, gravel, boardwalk and wooden steps. There are places where it is rough underfoot and/or exposed to steep terrain nearby, and greater care will be needed. As with all tracks of this type, a walking pole is recommended.

NOTE: This is a track to be completed *only* during the open season unless you have specific winter mountaineering equipment and knowledge. In winter it will become covered in snow, and avalanches are likely. Ill-equipped and inexperienced trampers have been killed and injured here during the off season.

A view over the south fiord of Lake Te Anau.

START POINT: Te Anau
END POINT: Te Anau
DISTANCE: 64 km
TIME: 2–4 days
SEASON: 25 October – 3 May
GRADING: Moderate fitness required
DOC HUTS: Luxmore (54 bunks), Iris Burn (50 bunks), Moturau (40 bunks)
DOC CAMPSITES: Brod Bay (15 sites), Iris Burn (15 sites)

RECOMMENDED TRIP OPTION: Take the full four days, staying at Luxmore Hut first, then Iris Burn and Moturau. This gives you plenty of time to recover and explore.

The alpine section of the track follows a circuitous route along ridge tops.

PLANNING

ACCESS: There are three beginning and ending points: the Fiordland National Park Visitor Centre in Te Anau, the Kepler Track car park near the control gates to Lake Te Anau, and Rainbow Reach between Lake Te Anau and Lake Manapōuri. Access to each is either by walking, or driving a short distance by road. Shuttle buses provide a daily service to all entry and exit points on the track during the Great Walks season, and a scheduled boat service also offers transport to Brod Bay. The best way to start the track is arguably from Te Anau township, and the route described in the chapter follows this option.

ACCOMMODATION, FOOD AND EQUIPMENT: Te Anau has a full range of accommodation options and is a lovely place to spend the night.

Stock up on everything you need for walking the track before you leave Te Anau. There is also a decent selection of cafes and restaurants for carbo-loading beforehand and a celebratory meal afterwards.

Descending from the upper section of the track.

The track between Iris Burn Hut and Moturau Hut.

WEATHER: While this area gets much less rainfall than Milford Sound (see Milford Track chapter), the higher, open section of the track is particularly exposed to what will sometimes be extreme mountain weather (strong winds, rain and snow). Check the forecast beforehand, and ask at the visitor centre or one of the DOC officers stationed at the huts if you are unsure about conditions ahead.

TRACK CONDITIONS: The middle portion of this track crosses an alpine environment and should be treated with the appropriate level of respect and caution. It is exposed to high winds, low visibility and the possibility of snow at any time of year. In poor conditions it may be advisable to turn around rather than risk the crossing – ask a DOC officer if you are unsure.

The lower portions of the track are generally maintained to a high standard and easy to complete in most conditions.

ROUTE DESCRIPTION

Te Anau to Kepler Track car park: 30 mins, 2 km

Starting in Te Anau, take the easy angled path that begins outside the Fiordland National Park Visitor Centre and winds its way around the lake shoreline. You will pass by the Te Anau Bird Sanctuary (well worth a visit afterwards), and then carry on along the edge of the lake to the point where the Kepler Track car park is situated near the Lake Te Anau control gates.

Kepler Track car park to Brod Bay: 1.5 hrs, 5 km

Cross the control gates, which offer a scenic photographic opportunity back towards the town of Te Anau, and then continue with easy walking through the beech and podocarp forest that pushes up against the shore of the lake. In places there are large beds of ferns covering the ground. Here and there you will get views of the lake, and a comprehensive trapping programme means you are likely to hear birdsong as you walk. Brod Bay and the first campsite are set in a grove of trees near the shore.

Brod Bay to Luxmore Hut: 3–6 hrs, 8 km

The climb begins. From Brod Bay, begin your ascent towards Luxmore Hut. At first the angle is gentle, but eventually it steepens to a more noticeable gradient. Occasionally there is a view through the forest canopy of the land falling away beneath your feet, but mostly you are cocooned within mature trees and regrowth. Pace yourself – it's a steady climb – and partway up you will be rewarded with a traverse under impressive limestone bluffs, cliffs that were once at the bottom of the ocean. Past the bluffs, the angle of the track relents just a little. The forest changes also, with gnarly and stunted trunks of mountain beech the predominant variety.

Luxmore Hut is a good place to hear and see kea, but please don't feed them.

The top of the bushline comes almost as a surprise. Carry on through fields of alpine grasses in the knowledge you are now less than an hour away from Luxmore Hut, your stop for the first night.

Luxmore Cave is a worthwhile side trip only 10 minutes' walk from the hut, but you will need a decent head torch to venture in past the cave's entrance.

Some of the alpine scenery, including Mt Luxmore, on the highest part of the track.

Luxmore Hut to Iris Burn Hut: 5–6 hrs, 14 km

Be warned! The next portion of the Kepler is about as spectacular as you are likely to find in New Zealand with such a well-formed track. Yes, it will feel as though you are starting your day on top of the world, and the feeling only gets better as you continue ascending towards the nearby summit of Mt Luxmore (1472 m), the highest point of the track. The South Fiord of Lake Te Anau winds its way past the Murchison Mountains (home to the very rare and quite enigmatic South Island takahē) beneath your feet. Above you is the rock-strewn dome of Mt Luxmore. It's only a short detour from the track to the summit, and well worth the effort. Take your camera.

Back on the main track, carry on along what feels like the very tops of the mountains, sometimes traversing rocky scree slopes and at other times staying on the spine of narrow ridge lines. There are two shelters to rest at and refuel from supplies in your pack, before a series of wooden steps and a steep, thigh-tiring descent through the forest eventually bring you to Iris Burn Hut. The hut is set in an open grassy field not far from the Iris Burn River and the second campsite.

Iris Burn Hut to Moturau Hut: 5–6 hrs, 17 km

Start this day knowing all of the hard climbing is behind you. Instead, enjoy the changing scenery through open grasslands and more peaceful forest as the track takes you over a low saddle, then down past the old scar of a large slip. Stop for a moment and consider just how dynamic landscapes such as this can be. Pass by a shelter at Rocky Point, and then enter the lowland beech and podocarp forest and a gradually sloped gorge. When you reach the shore of Lake Manapōuri, you will almost certainly want to stop and take more photos. This is a soothing part of the track, winding easily through forest and ferns, with the lapping of water always on your right.

Moturau Hut, set on the shore of the lake, offers evening sunsets that will have you braving the sandflies for as long as you can with your camera.

Moturau Hut to Rainbow Reach: 1.5–2 hrs, 6 km

This is your last day on the track, and the going is easy. The route takes you through forest and sometimes across a boardwalked area of fragile wetland. Along the way you'll encounter plenty of inquisitive bird life; it may seem

Iris Burn Hut.

as though the fantails are chasing you, but in fact they are after any insects you may have stirred up as you pass by. The track then follows the Waiau River terrace, where a long swing bridge crosses to Rainbow Reach (if that is where you are finishing). You can leave the track here and catch a shuttle bus to Te Anau, but it is worth walking the final section to complete the full circuit.

Rainbow Reach to Te Anau: 3–5 hrs, 12 km

The last stretch of the track continues easily along forested terraces above the Waiau River. The trees are mostly mountain and red beech, and there is an area of mānuka scrubland, which once belonged to an early run-holder, Jack Beer. The bird life here is plentiful, and the calls of bellbirds will likely echo through the trees above as you make your way back to the car park near the control gates, before following the final lakeside path back to the DOC visitor centre at Te Anau.

POINTS OF INTEREST

The scale of a lake

Realising the size of Lake Te Anau may be difficult while standing beside the lake edge. Stretching 65 kilometres north to south, it has three main fiords, which are recognised as the only inland fiords in New Zealand. Walking the Kepler Track, especially above Luxmore Hut, gives you a much better perspective, especially of the South Fiord.

A call to action

Lake Te Anau provides power via the Manapōuri hydroelectric power station in its West Arm. Water is discharged through two 10 kilometre-long tailrace tunnels, which head to Doubtful Sound and the sea. Back in 1959, the government proposed raising Lake Manapōuri's water level by 30 metres, which would join it to Lake Te Anau and turn the two bodies of water into a 'super lake'. The overall aim was to generate enough hydro power for the development of a new aluminium smelter in Southland.

What followed was nothing short of national outrage: people the length of New Zealand were stunned at the proposal to alter beyond recognition one of the country's most scenic lakes. The 'Save Manapouri' campaign lasted more than a decade, before the government finally yielded to the pressure and halted its plans for raising the lake. The success of the campaign is regarded as a milestone in the history of New Zealand's environmental protection movement.

Kepler Challenge

Every year, around 450 runners tackle the Kepler Challenge Mountain Run over the full length of the Kepler Track. The event has been held since 1988, and draws competitors from throughout New Zealand and around the world. Typically a number of competitors will complete the course in less than 5 hours, with others taking up to 11 hours. The fastest time to date was set in 2013 by Martin Dent, who ran it in 4 hours, 33 minutes and 37 seconds.

The optional crossing of the Waiau River.

Kids Restore the Kepler

Kids Restore the Kepler is a fantastic programme involving local schools and other educational institutions, along with the Fiordland Conservation Trust and DOC. Launched in 2011, the project focuses on bringing back more native birds to the area, including greater numbers of mohua (yellowhead), rifleman, South Island kākā and kiwi. The project uses traps to kill rats, possums and stoats, and currently there are over 500 set in an area of around 3000 hectares. It is hoped that the Kepler Peninsula will in time become a mainland island sanctuary for at-risk species.

The plight of the kea

New Zealand and the world's only alpine parrot – also considered to be the planet's most intelligent bird – is under threat. Loss of habitat, predation from introduced pests, and even well-meaning but ill-informed humans are causing the kea population to decline sharply. During your travels, please note that it is important not to feed kea as this encourages bad habits, and over time they lose the ability to fend for themselves.

Lake Manapōuri.

OFF THE TRACK

Your legs may be tired after completing the Kepler, but this area is too special not to take the opportunity to keep exploring.

Te Anau Bird Sanctuary

Set on the shore of Lake Te Anau, the bird sanctuary is an easy 10 minute walk from the Fiordland National Park Visitor Centre. It is open all day, with free entry (although a gold coin donation is appreciated). Here you will be able to see endangered native birds including the takahē and kākā.

Te Anau Caves boat trip

The Te Anau caves system is set on the western shore of the lake. Enjoy the delicate glowworm grotto and other experiences by guided boat trip across the lake and back from Te Anau.

Dusky Track

If, after completing the Kepler, you are looking for a much more challenging tramp, the nearby Dusky Track is worth considering. Despite being only 20 kilometres longer than the Kepler, the Dusky can take up to 8–10 days to complete – an indication of how much more rugged the terrain is. The track crosses two ranges of mountains and traverses three major valleys between Lake Hauroko and Lake Manapōuri. You should be prepared for anything: some sections of the track may even become impassable due to flooding after heavy rain, a situation that is not uncommon in this area. The Dusky Track is recommended only for experienced, well-equipped groups with high levels of fitness.

Tuatapere Hump Ridge Track

A little further away, in Southland, this 3 day guided circuit takes you along the south coast of New Zealand and up to the subalpine Hump Ridge. The guided trip is not a cheap option, but for those with the money it is well worth doing for the experience of luxury tramping. Book online at www.humpridgetrack.co.nz.

RAKIURA TRACK

A LAND *ALMOST* FORGOTTEN

The first and last days of the track stay close to the coast and estuary.

RAKIURA TRACK

A LAND *ALMOST* FORGOTTEN // 32 KM, 2–3 DAYS

— HIGHLIGHTS

- Tackle the least busy of the Great Walks.
- Explore a varied terrain of intimate coastline, lush rainforest and sheltered estuary backwaters.
- Spot abundant bird life, including large flocks of the gregarious kākā and parakeets.
- Encounter remnants of early Māori and Pākehā history, as well as the power of nature to reassert itself over early human impact.
- Grab a chance to hear, track, and maybe even spot New Zealand's elusive national bird, the kiwi.

THE HARDEST-TO-REACH CORNERS of New Zealand tend to be that way for a good reason. Few people succeed in getting themselves to the remotest southern and western edges of Stewart Island/Rakiura – places that could be described quite literally as nearing the ends of the earth. This farthest corner of Rakiura presents an exposed, rainswept landscape, with not much to be seen across the rocky outcrops and low-slung headlands other than ocean swells coming to pound the coastline and a southern horizon leading away to Antarctica. Other than knowing that you are in the most isolated part of the country, there seems little worthy of appreciation.

A few kilometres away as the kererū flies, and tucked into the much more sheltered and forgiving northern aspect of New Zealand's third-largest island, the Rakiura Track is an accessible and gentler introduction to the island.

Imagine native birdsong that is sometimes so loud and boisterous, you may struggle to hear yourself breathe. Walk through areas of ancient rainforest, the trees tall and dark, and all around you an undergrowth seemingly so impenetrable that to stray far from the trail leaves you feeling as though you might never return to civilisation. Consider the longest days

N
Big Bungaree Beach
Port William
Magnetic Bch
Port William / Potirepo
Peters Point
Maori Beach
Lee
Bay
Horseshoe Bay
North Arm
Halfmoon Bay
(Oban)
Halfmoon Bay
Fern Gully
Sawdust Bay
Ryans Creek
Track
Thule Bay
Kidney Fern Arm
Kaipipi Bay
Prices Inlet
Ulva Island
Paterson Inlet / Whaka ā Te Wera
0
5
10 km

imaginable in the height of summer, and clear nights when you just might be lucky enough to catch sight of aurora australis, the fantastical Southern Lights.

Stewart Island/Rakiura seems to be a place that many New Zealanders might have wondered about for much of their lives, but few actually take the time to explore. Perhaps you, too, have kept the imagining of it in the recess of your mind, from time to time wondering 'if only'. Well, here is your chance. Completing the Rakiura Track is an opportunity to experience a part of this country that is unique in so many ways.

TRACK DETAILS

LOCATION: Stewart Island/Rakiura, Southland

TRACK TYPE: This is a circular route that can be walked in either direction from the settlement of Oban. The terrain is undulating, with little altitude gain (around 300 m), and passes through a mix of sandy coastline, rainforest and estuarine backwaters, as well as sites of historical interest. Parts of the track cross Māori land, and access has been granted courtesy of the owners.

START POINT: Lee Bay (5 km easy walk to/from Oban)
END POINT: Fern Gully (2 km easy walk from/to Oban)

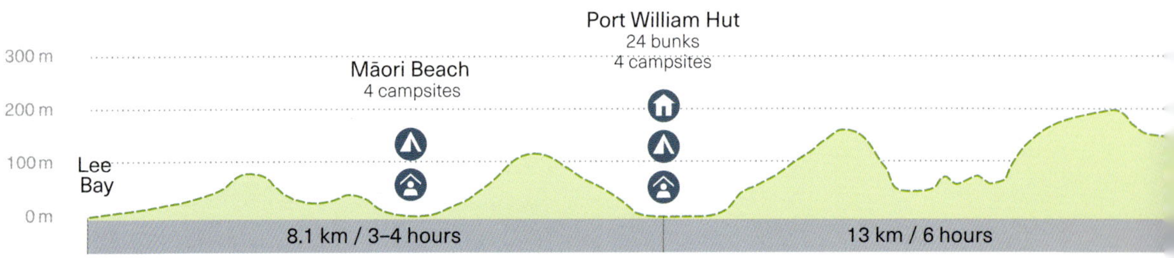

The chain 'linking' Stewart Island with the South Island, which can be seen at the start of the track.

hut campsite shelter

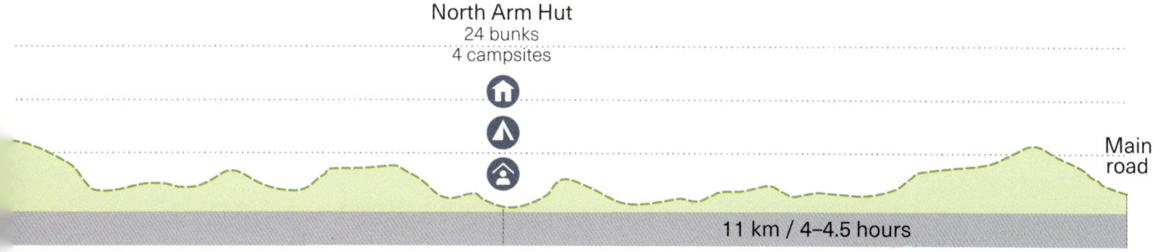

DISTANCE: 32 km
TIME: 2–3 days
SEASON: Any time of year, due to the area's temperate climate (winter is often cool, rather than cold, especially when compared to the South Island)
GRADING: Easy/moderate fitness required
DOC HUTS: Port William (24 bunks), North Arm (24 bunks)
DOC CAMPSITES: Māori Beach (4 sites), Port William (4 sites), North Arm (4 sites). Note, the campsites are not next to the huts.

RECOMMENDED TRIP OPTION: Although this walk can be done in a long day, it is recommended you take 3 (starting at Lee Bay and finishing at Fern Gully) and enjoy the bird life and the island's gentle pace.

PLANNING

ACCESS: A one hour ferry crossing from Bluff, or a 20 minute plane ride from Invercargill.

Be warned: the adventure may begin before you even reach Stewart Island/Rakiura! The South Island coastal town of Bluff and its residents tend to hunker down in the lee of Motupōhue, or Bluff Hill, whenever a south-westerly wind whips across the exposed Foveaux Strait. In these conditions, the ferry crossing to Rakiura will be rather bumpy (as can be the plane ride). But there are plenty of comfortable seats inside the cabin. Or, if you prefer, you can stand outside near the stern, hang on and watch swells roll past and plumes of spray breaking over the hull; as the South Island slowly recedes from sight, perhaps beneath a layer of cloud — ahead, everything but the low headlands of your destination remains elusive.

ACCOMMODATION, FOOD AND EQUIPMENT: There are a number of accommodation options in the main settlement of Oban and nearby, including rental baches, motels, hotels, B&Bs, cabins and a campground. During the busy summer period especially it will pay to book before you arrive.

There is a local pub and cafe in Oban, and some other small eateries,

An Oban local.

which may or may not be open depending on the time of year and the owner's preference. A local shop stocks most basic food items as well as other supplies needed for the track. It is recommended you eat blue cod and chips at the local pub at least once (particularly if a rugby game is on the television). This is a quintessential Stewart Island experience, especially if you want to rub shoulders with a few of the 400 or so locals. Most tourists go to the cafe for dinner, but the pub is much more fun, especially so at the completion of your tramp to cap off a great trip. It's a real social melting pot, and likely to be busy on any night of the week.

WEATHER: Without a sheltering mountain range, Stewart Island/Rakiura is certainly exposed to wind and rain. And when a storm hits this southern corner of New Zealand it tends to have the volume turned up. That said, the island generally has a temperate climate, and any bad weather often passes through quite quickly. The annual rainfall at Oban is comparable to that

An old milling site near Māori Beach.

of Auckland, and much lower than on the western side of Stewart Island/ Rakiura. Hence, the Rakiura Track will likely be more pleasant and sheltered than, say, the longer and much more challenging North West Circuit. Still, as is the case with many other parts of New Zealand, you should be prepared for prolonged periods of wet and stormy weather.

TRACK CONDITIONS: Generally speaking, the Rakiura Track is clearly marked and well maintained, with a mix of gravel and boardwalk in places as well as uncovered soil and sand. It is undulating, with only small hill climbs, especially when compared to some of the other Great Walks. Sometimes – and this is a reflection of the nature of the land as well as the rainfall this area receives – there may be small sections that are rough, steep and muddy. A walking pole is recommended for anyone who finds slippery conditions underfoot challenging.

TRACK DESCRIPTION

Optional walk from Oban to Lee Bay (start of track): 1.5 hrs, 5 km

This is an easy amble along the edge of a sealed road, passing by local homes, cribs and the quiet Horseshoe Bay, which faces north-east. It is a pleasant way to start your journey as you ease into the laid-back local lifestyle, enjoying the fact that not one single tourist bus will pass you by. Leaving the coast for a short time, you take a bush-lined gravel road over a saddle, and then down to Lee Bay and the start of the track proper.

Lee Bay to Māori Beach: 2 hrs, 5 km

Passing by the chain-link sculpture at Lee Bay, a symbol linking Stewart Island/Rakiura with the South Island (there is another similar sculpture at Bluff), the track follows an easy terrace through rejuvenating bush a few metres above the coastline. In places it opens out to offer views to the north and the distant outline of the South Island across Foveaux Strait.

Below you are sheltered coves and rocky headlands, home to many of the island's coastal birds. In places at low tide it is possible to walk around small sections of the coast and pick up the track again at various locations, before rejoining the track permanently to continue around Peters Point and on to the long, sandy sweep of Māori Beach.

At the southern end of Māori Beach, which was once the site of a Māori village, the small creek can easily be waded at low tide. At high tide, however, it is perhaps more prudent to keep your footwear dry by staying on the path until you come to another footbridge. Here, a side track leads off to a rusting steam boiler, a relic from the old sawmill days. In the early 1900s, a small but viable timber-milling industry developed here, and by 1920 there were two sawmills, a permanent population and even a school. The enterprise lasted until around 1930.

For those wishing to end their first day here, the Māori Beach Campsite is situated in a sheltered clearing tucked in behind the sand dunes, close to the white-sand beach and near its southern end.

Māori Beach to Port William Hut: 1–1.5 hrs, 3 km

The walk along Māori Beach is a good chance to take your footwear off and feel the sand between your toes. This is a sheltered stretch of coast and, on a warm day, also perhaps worth a swim.

At the northern end of Māori Beach a swing bridge gets you across the small estuary to the start of a gradual ascent up a forested hill. You will reach an intersection in the track where there is the option of heading directly to North Arm, but instead you turn right and carry on to the coast and a campsite near Magnetic Beach in Port William. Port William Hut is sited on an open grassy clearing just a few minutes further along the track beyond the campsite.

Port William was originally the site of the Māori settlement of Pā Whakataka, and a number of nearby bays were used as hunting camps and reached by waka (canoe).

The headland beyond Port William created a natural harbour base for European sealers and whalers in the early nineteenth century. Prospecting for gold proved unsuccessful, as did a government-subsidised programme to settle Shetland Island emigrants during the 1870s, which lasted little more than a year.

Port William Hut to North Arm Hut: 6 hrs, 13 km

Backtrack a pleasant 40 minutes or so through forest to the turn-off you passed the previous day, and continue on to North Arm. On this section of track you will pass beneath a variety of native vegetation, including areas of previously milled forest as well as virgin podocarp trees. There are more remnants of milling activity at various points, as the route sometimes follows the old tramlines that were once used for extracting giant logs from the forest. It may come as something of a relief to realise that forests like this can recover, and indeed flourish, after such human impact. Indeed, much of this section will more likely reinforce a sense of awe at the stillness of the forest and, especially, at the giant trees still remaining. And you may begin to feel, if not complete isolation, then certainly a growing sense that you are travelling near the heart of an ancient land.

Most of the trail is undulating, and in some places likely to be muddy. You will be accompanied by birdsong in the trees, and possibly catch sight of the whitetail deer as they dart for cover. (Introduced species are relatively low in

Port William Hut.

number on Stewart Island, which is renowned for being free of many of the predators – such as ferrets, weasels and stoats – that plague our bird life on both the South and North islands.)

When you finally reach North Arm Hut, this is a peaceful location to relax and recover, explore the coast's nooks and crannies, perhaps go for a swim, and then watch a colourful sunset over lowlands to the west.

North Arm Hut to Fern Gully car park: 4 hrs, 11 km

Paterson Inlet is a huge tidal estuary that stretches inland from near the eastern edge of Stewart Island/Rakiura. Its various arms provide sheltered waterborne access to other, far more remote parts of the island, and the Rakiura Track curves along the edge of its northern shoreline.

Passing mostly through forest but also dropping down to small, secluded bays, the track sidles around various headlands to Sawdust Bay. It passes another sawmill site, which was in operation between 1914 and 1918, and then continues through a lovely section of forest dominated by rimu and kāmahi, with long 'old man's beard' mosses drooping from the tree branches. Emerging at the picturesque bays of Kidney Fern Arm and then Kaipipi, you

The long sweep of Māori Beach.

The cheeky kākā.

may see more remnants of the two sawmills that operated here in the 1860s, at one stage employing more than 100 people in removing the local timber.

While the waters of Paterson Inlet sheltered whaling boats during the early settler days, the main industry here at the time was in timber. Later, in the 1920s, the Norwegian Whaling Company ran a repair base in Prices Inlet, where harpooning chaser boats were stored and serviced in preparation for work during the Antarctic summers.

You are now close to completing the track, and the last section follows a wide, cobbled stretch of the former Kaipipi Road. There is a final descent through more forest to the Fern Gully car park, before the finish point a further 2 kilometres along the road verge to Oban.

For those with energy still in their legs, there is an option to carry on around the coastline to the east, following the Ryans Creek Track for another 1–1.5 hours to finish at Thule Bay, and from there walk back over the hill to Oban.

POINTS OF INTEREST

What's in a name?

For Māori, Stewart Island/Rakiura is Te Punga o Te Waka a Māui – the anchor for Māui's canoe (the South Island) as he hauled up the North Island. The anchor chain is represented by the chain-link sculpture by artist Russell Beck at Lee Bay.

These days Rakiura is the more commonly used Māori name, and translates as 'glowing skies', perhaps referring to the spectacular Southern Lights, the aurora australis, that can be seen here sometimes.

The English name comes from William Stewart, first officer on the *Pegasus*, a sealing ship that first sailed to the island from Australia in 1809. Stewart charted much of the area during a number of voyages over subsequent decades. As part of a 1998 Treaty of Waitangi settlement between Ngāi Tahu and the Crown, the name officially became Stewart Island/Rakiura.

For bird lovers

Most of the island is a bird-lover's dream, and not just because of the high likelihood of spotting kiwi. Along the coastline, look out for the muttonbird or sooty shearwater (considered a local delicacy), Cape pigeon, and various species of rare terns and shags. There are three penguin species living here (Fiordland, yellow-eyed/hoiho and little blue), and six species of albatross or mollymawk, along with petrels and, in winter, fairy prions.

In the forest, you may hear the beautiful calling of bellbirds and tūī, or be chased by fantails looking for flying insects. While these are common on both the North and South islands, the sheer number of songbirds here makes you realise what the rest of New Zealand used to be like. You may also see parakeets and shining cuckoos high in the trees, along with large flocks of kākā. And the wetlands here are home to the rare and secretive Stewart Island fernbird.

The tidal flats of Paterson Inlet are a haven for a variety of wading birds, including the New Zealand dotterel, oystercatchers, herons and godwits.

Kiwi watching: dos and don'ts

The kiwi mostly feeds at night and doesn't like to be disturbed. Look for a likely site during the day where there are lots of footprints and holes in the ground left by kiwi probing with their long beaks. Return at night, but be as quiet as possible, and use minimal torch light. Find a comfortable place to sit . . . and wait. You are likely to hear them calling and shuffling around at first, and if you are really lucky you may see their dark outline. Remember, they won't like a torch being shone on them (if you have a red light setting this isn't so bad) or the flash of a camera. In some more remote places on the island it is possible to see kiwi during the day.

Unique trees

The forest here incorporates the world's southernmost reach of podocarps and hardwoods, including an abundance of kāmahi, miro and rātā. But it is the ancient rimu that dominates much of the canopy. The observant will notice that there is a conspicuous absence of beech trees. This is because seeds would have been dispersed here by seabirds flying from the mainland. Beech seeds are usually dispersed by the wind, and so never made it this far south.

Being local

It has been said that Stewart Island residents tend to be rather quirky, with an odd sense of humour, and are keen to protect their low-key lifestyle. Perhaps only partially in jest, Stewart Islanders like to refer to their homeland as independent from the rest of New Zealand.

Looking at a map of the island, it seems that even the place names are quirky. In Paterson Inlet, islets include Moses Nugget, Dirty Island, Kidney Fern Island and the Faith, Hope and Charity Group.

The view from North Arm Hut.

OFF THE TRACK

As well as the Rakiura Track, there are plenty of other things worth seeing and doing here, whether you're in search of adventure or merely keen to embrace the slow pace of life. Most visitors focus their activities around the northern and eastern aspects of the island. Travelling to the largely untracked southern coast is better left to the truly adventurous.

Visit Ulva Island

Ulva Island is situated in Paterson Inlet, and is only a short boat ride from Oban. Covering an area of around 260 hectares, the heavily forested bird sanctuary was declared pest free in 1997 after an extensive eradication programme. Since then, it has developed into a safe haven for threatened native species and is a local tourist attraction.

Several species, including the South Island saddleback, mohua (yellowhead) and Stewart Island robin, have been reintroduced to Ulva, and today there are healthy populations of these birds, as well as the southern brown kiwi.

Travelling here and quietly walking beneath the forest, keeping an eye out for as many different species as you can and listening to the cacophony of birdsong that surrounds you is one of the special experiences of visiting this part of New Zealand.

Explore Paterson Inlet

You used to be able to hire kayaks to experience this, but these days you need a guide. Which is probably fair enough, given the changeable weather and sea conditions. Having a guide means you will be safer, as well as taken to all of the best spots. Money well spent! And for those less inclined to exercise, there are boats available for charter.

Climb Mt Anglem / Hananui

While Anglem/Hananui is not a particularly high or technical mountain, to climb it is not without challenges (and certainly a step up from the Rakiura Track). Getting the weather right is one thing. A full day's walk from Oban (10-plus hours, and be prepared for thigh-deep mud puddles!) brings you to Christmas Village Hut. This is part of the North West Circuit. From near the hut another track leads up the northern slopes of Anglem. Once out of the bush you are certainly exposed to the elements, but the view is unrivalled. The summit is mostly devoid of growth: other than a few boulders, lichens and mosses, it seems more like a moonscape.

Tramp the North West Circuit

As indicated by its name, the North West Circuit circumnavigates the north-western corner of the island. At 120 kilometres in length, this rugged trail takes 8–10 days to complete, passing through some of New Zealand's most remote yet still tracked terrain. The circuit is on the bucket list of many serious trampers. But be warned: this is a big step up from the Rakiura Track and, if the Great Walk is one of your first back-country tracks, you would be advised to do some other intermediate trips before tackling the full North West Circuit.

A less challenging but still rewarding option is to charter a flight to the western side of the island (it lands on the beach at Mason Bay) and hike the last, easier few days of the circuit through to North Arm Hut and then on to Oban.

On Stewart Island/
Rakiura you are never
far from the forest.

Milford Track needs ongoing care to keep it pristine.

GIVING BACK TO THE ENVIRONMENT

If you enjoyed your experience on the Great Walks, be aware that there are many less well-known but equally awesome tramps to do throughout New Zealand. DOC will be able to give you ideas as well as a list of local tramping clubs and walking groups to join (these often organise specific trips).

But our beautiful environment is under threat. More than 4000 native New Zealand plants and animals are among the million species worldwide that are at risk of extinction, according to a report from the Intergovernmental Science Policy Platform on Biodiversity and Ecosystem Services (IPBES). More and more species will be lost within our lifetime if we don't intervene.

It's not just up to central government to halt this decline – protection and conservation are everyone's responsibility. The value and importance of community conservation efforts, public–private partnerships and philanthropic support can't be stated strongly enough. This means working together with iwi, public and private resource managers, community-based restoration groups and landowners to try to achieve the admirable goal of a pest-free New Zealand by 2050.

Regardless of whether you are a Kiwi or an overseas visitor, there are many ways you can give back to our great outdoors. These range from donations to non-profit organisations, to volunteering for one of the many great environmental programmes that exist.

It is also possible for you to directly assist scientific researchers. By sharing any sightings of particular species during your time in the outdoors, you can help them better understand threatened populations. The NatureWatch website (www.naturewatch.org.nz) explains how this process works, and information on particular species of interest can also be found in some of the huts as well as local DOC offices.

If you live in New Zealand, planting native trees and setting traps on your own land is a great way to help protect bird life. There are various local community groups involved in predator control at local parks and reserves and they always need more volunteers. Check out the section on the DOC website about volunteer pest control and home-trapping options.

USEFUL WEBSITES

Adventure Smart, www.adventuresmart.nz – helps you stay safe in the great outdoors.

Department of Conservation, www.doc.govt.nz – your go-to site for information on all of the Great Walks.

Federated Mountain Clubs, www.fmc.org.nz – useful site linking various clubs and organisations related to the outdoors and mountains.

Leave No Trace (New Zealand), www.leavenotrace.org.nz – informative site offering advice on interacting with our outdoors in a sustainable way.

MetService, www.metservice.com – provides forecasts and extreme weather warnings.

Metvuw, www.metvuw.com – provides weather forecast charts up to seven days in advance.

NatureWatch, www.naturewatch.org.nz – educational and useful bio-recording site, where you can upload sightings of flora and fauna.

NZ Mountain Safety Council, www.mountainsafety.org.nz – provides lots of information for outdoor enthusiasts.

NZ Land Search and Rescue, www.landsar.org.nz – a national volunteer organisation providing land-based rescue support.

INDEX

The final resting place of many a tired boot and shoe on the Heaphy Track.

ACKNOWLEDGEMENTS

It took a combined effort to bring this book together. Thanks to the team at Penguin Random House: Jeremy Sherlock, Rachel Clark and Sarah Yankelowitz.

Thanks to Chris and Andrew and everyone at Bivouac Outdoor for their long-term support with high-quality outdoor equipment and clothing.

Thanks to Phillip and Kirsty at Canoe Safaris based in Ōhakune for ensuring the logistical support around our trip on the Whanganui River ran smoothly.

And thanks to the Department of Conservation for keeping the tracks and huts on the Great Walks so well maintained.